CW00750017

A PEOPLE'S HISTORY OF WOODCRAFT FOLK

Phineas Harper
Jonny Helm

Δ

Paul Bemrose
Doug Bourn
Kit Jones
Saskia Neibig
Jon Nott
Annebella Pollen
Martin Pover
Nicola Samson
Zoë Waterman
Joel White

▽

Foreword by Jeremy Corbyn

Published by Woodcraft Folk in London
ISBN 978-1-873695-11-1

Written, designed and edited by Phineas Harper
Photography by Jonny Helm

Printed and bound by Biddles Ltd. Kings Lynn.
Supported with funds from the Heritage Lottery
Fund and the Arts and Humanities Research Council.

Arts & Humanities
Research Council

heritage
lottery fund

LOTTERY FUNDED

For the thousands of
Woodcraft Folk leaders
through whose dedication,
creativity and friendship,
generations of young
people have found their
voice and power

Contents

Foreword
Jeremy Corbyn MP

Camping with Woodcraft Folk all over Britain and in Finland has given me some of the happiest and most fulfilling times of my life.

Whenever I come away from a Woodcraft Folk camp I feel a sense of rejuvenation and invigoration, having met hundreds of young people who share the values of internationalism, global justice and co-operation which are profoundly needed to create a more peaceful, sustainable and fair world.

Since its inception in 1925, Woodcraft Folk has actively campaigned against all forms of war, racism and inequality. Woodcraft Folk lead by example, whether in their camps in the UK or through their unique youth work here and around the world. They helped orchestrate the Kindertransport, rescuing many Jewish children from Nazi Germany. They campaigned against apartheid in South Africa and marched against war in Iraq. They have fought for the rights of LGBT people and oppressed minorities of all backgrounds. Above all they have supported and empowered many thousands of young people to explore big ideas, develop new skills and make lifelong friends.

Woodcraft Folk members are inspiring individuals giving their energy week after week to educate the next generation of scientists, teachers, artists and activists. They open our minds to better ways of doing things. Their green shirts and parachute games are regular sights, whether playing games in a village hall, camping by a lake or marching past the House of Commons.

This book marks the 90th birthday of this remarkable organisation. Long may Woodcraft Folk thrive.

Preface
Jon Nott

My involvement with Woodcraft Folk began when my step-daughter started going to the local Pioneer group (10-12 year olds) in 2006. After two years of steadfastly declaring myself 'too busy to volunteer', I was persuaded in 2008 to accompany a group of Venturers (13-15 year olds) as they represented our district at Annual Gathering and proposed a motion about fair trade. From that moment I was hooked. Within two years I had applied for the post of General Secretary – and been appointed by an interview panel ranging in age from ten to 60.

Six years on, the process of bringing this book into being, and indeed, our entire 90th anniversary project has been a wonderful journey into the roots of Woodcraft Folk. Along the way I have learnt much about the inspirational founders and early leaders of Woodcraft Folk and our precursor organisations. I have come to a deeper understanding of the movement's core principles and seen how, though the practice changes through the decades, all of our activities are underpinned by the same values, which shine through the wide range of Woodcraft Folk experiences.

This book provides a series of snapshots of our movement through the years and shows the wide variety of ways in which our founding principles were, and continue to be, lived by generations of children and young people.

Woodcraft Folk has always been at the forefront of inclusion – in 1925 the idea of girls and boys camping and playing together was still far from the norm. Since then, Woodcraft Folk has campaigned against racism, worked for the equal treatment of LGBT people and, in partnership with other organisations, has offered a Woodcraft Folk experience to those disabled by society's attitude to difference. As a result many children who have not felt welcome in formal education or establishment youth organisations have found a home in Woodcraft Folk.

A vision of international peace – spanning the world with friendship – has had many different interpretations, from the fun of international camps and cultural exchanges, such as the iconic

Brighton international camps in 1937 (page 72) and 1946 (page 92 and, most recently, 2011's CoCamp (page 184) to the harsh reality and practical solidarity of the Kindertransport, explored in detail by Saskia Neibig on page 86.

And 'woodcraft' itself – the skills of living in harmony with nature – encompasses the inter-war movement to open up the countryside to young urban workers, the more recent environmental campaigns embodied in 2001's Sust 'n' Able international camp (page 174) and the resurgence of practical bushcraft skills, in many cases virtually unchanged from the time of Ernest Thompson Seton.

Our adoption of co-operative principles and links with the co-operative movement run through the organisation's life, underpinning our internal democracy, the way we organise camps and plan group nights, and providing numerous avenues for young people to continue to live out the values of Woodcraft Folk as workers, consumers and citizens. One of my predecessors as General Secretary, Doug Bourn, looks at these aspects on page 134.

Finally, what I believe makes Woodcraft Folk truly radical is that, from the very start, Woodcraft Folk has been run by and with young people rather than simply for young people. The idea that from their first session as a young Woodchip (under 6s), a child can spend a lifetime in this organisation and be sure that throughout their voice will always not just be heard, but will carry as much weight as any other individual is almost unique. In Woodcraft Folk at all times that child will have genuine agency at whatever level they engage.

I hope that in this book you will find, as did I, things to celebrate, to inspire, to make you laugh and to spur you to action. And I hope that you will join us as we head for our centenary and continue to go singing to the fashioning of a new world.

Blue Skies

Introduction
Phineas Harper

Remember the good old days? The golden years when the world was smaller. Remember when children respected their elders and betters? Were seen and not heard? Knew the value of a pound and weren't afraid of a hard day's work? The clichés which adults trot out to glorify their past selves at the expense of the youth of the day are so well trodden they feel absurd. Yet the pastime of deriding the young never seems to grow old. Kids on the street: more must be done to tackle gang warfare. Kids inside: internet addiction is out of control. Kid sitting alone: depression epidemic. Kid running around: ADHD epidemic. Kid aces exams: standards are slipping. Kid flunks exams: no aspiration. The conditions the young endure are invariably a playground for adult moral grandstanding. Even in the youth work sector the assumptions and tastes of well-meaning adults often smother any possibility of child-led self-determination.

It is illuminating to look to the earliest years of Woodcraft Folk when Leslie Paul (page 22), not yet 20, and his peers founded the organisation. Their achievements at such a young age might seem astonishing but they thrived due to the freedom they enjoyed – freedom to test themselves and their ideas without adults framing the limits of their ambition. For those who believe the voice of children is worth listening to, Woodcraft Folk has blazed a trail throughout the 20th century, supporting and empowering young people of all backgrounds without patronising. Scouts today looks much as early Woodcraft Folk did: co-educational, secular, open to gay and straight alike. This book explores a history told through objects and their stories of this remarkable organisation that has touched so many lives. It is a people's history as remembered, affirmed and interpreted by the members of Woodcraft Folk. Not seeking to be comprehensive nor academic, it instead offers glimpses into the many chapters of Woodcraft Folk's evolution, struggles and adventures.

In creating this book it became quickly obvious that the teaching philosophy and practice of Woodcraft Folk has radically changed over 90 years of incremental democratic adjustment. At a surface-level glance it seems rigorous, skills-based teaching has slowly been chipped away, supplanted with liberal self-expressive play, with the occasional dose of politics thrown in. There are some kernels of truth in this interpretation of Woodcraft Folk history that raise challenging questions the movement should consider. But it is also a reading inevitably pinned to romanticising the past, and subjective assumptions over what constitutes effort and valuable output. Changes in technology, for example, have had a huge impact on the pedagogy of the organisation. In the 1920s camping was difficult, time consuming and unusual. Official campsites were few and far between. There were no ubiquitous music festivals and tent technology was poor with the consumer market growing but small. Cash-strapped Woodcraft Folk groups couldn't simply buy discount tents from a Millets - they had to make them from scratch. In Basil Rawson's 1946 publication *The Woodcraft Way*, one page shows a pattern for making a rucksack as most members once would – hard, time consuming work but necessary. Seen through the rose-tinted lens of nostalgia we imagine strapping Woodcraft Folk youths able to survive in the wilderness, fashioning tools from their environment. It is an appealing image and was a powerful practice – working class children were born into a social status that ran deep. The act of taking a young person out of the city to camp in the countryside and equipping them with the right tool (whether a knife or an idea) to command agency in the world alongside equal peers was transformative in itself. Politics wasn't an activity enacted at Woodcraft Folk – it was Woodcraft Folk.

Today the world and its challenges have changed. It is true that the hand craftsmanship evident in early Woodcraft Folk artefacts is gone and the Woodcraft Folk curriculum is more relaxed but this stems from fundamental pragmatism which has moved with the times. What would be the value in making a rucksack from scratch when lighter, stronger alternatives are mass-produced? You may no longer find a young member carving linocuts (page 60) but instead they might be shooting a film, developing a website, planning direct action protest or publishing a book. The rigour Woodcraft Folk still embodies is in unflinching compassion for humankind, and that will never diminish.

With Light of Knowledge in their eyes!

ROYAL ARSENAL CO-OPERATIVE SOCIETY Ltd.

—— EDUCATION DEPARTMENT. ——

BOOK SELLERS.

CO-OPERATIVE INSTITUTE,
PARSONS HILL, WOOLWICH, S.E. 18.

Secretary: JOSEPH REEVES.
Telephone No.: WOOLWICH 2121.

Our Ref. _____ JR/MB.

Your Ref. _____

9th May, 1925.

Dear Mr. Paul,

      I have pleasure in informing you that my Committee have decided to make a grant of £5.0.0. for camping equipment for the Wayfarers' Fellowship. They make this grant on condition that all camping equipment purchased out of this grant remains the property of the Department.

      I enclose herewith a letter which if presented to Mr. Benn, Furnishing Manager at Woolwich, will make it possible to purchase the goods through our co-operative agency.

        Yours fraternally,

          Secretary,

Mr. Leslie A. Paul.
   4, Bovill Road.
      FOREST HILL.

Grant

This letter arguably marks the dawn of Woodcraft Folk. It confirms a £5 grant (£270 in today's money) for camping equipment made out to the first ever Woodcraft Folk group, the Wayfarers Fellowship, 9 May 1925

Photo
A young Woodcraft
Folk member focuses
on constructing a fire.
Members were trained
to be able to build a
wide variety of fire
structures suited to
different circumstances

Kindred of the Kibbo Kift

The people and practices that preceded Woodcraft Folk

Annebella Pollen

Woodcraft Folk has been profoundly shaped by the preceding organisations of which its early members had been a part. Both of Woodcraft Folk's co-founders, Leslie Paul (page 22) and the often-forgotten Sidney Shaw, had been Kinsfolk of Kibbo Kift, a co-educational, all-ages outdoor organisation that had utopian ambitions to bring world peace through camping, hiking, handicraft and ritual. Kibbo Kift had been founded by the artist, author and Scout Commissioner John 'White Fox' Hargrave in 1920 in reaction to his increasing dissatisfaction with the militarism and imperialism of Scouts which he saw as drifting away from its core woodcraft principles (in this context meaning nature study and outdoor skills). When Hargrave was expelled from Scouts for his public criticisms of its founder Robert Baden

A Kibbo Kift
Herald's surcoat,
worn for ceremonial
announcements, c.1923

Powell, he took with him many pacifist Scout groups, combining them with the free thinkers and creative practitioners he had met through his interests in progressive education, comparative religion and the arts.

Kibbo Kift – the name meant 'proof of strength' – was seen by many socialists as a corrective to scouting's problems. Hargrave's charisma as a leader and the group's colourful and mystical methods drew hundreds of followers, including the teenage Leslie 'Little Otter' Paul, who had first been first inspired by Hargrave's writings on the outdoor life at the tender age of 11. The Kibbo Kift covenant was committed to reorganising industry through a revival of craft practice, celebrating nature, spirituality and establishing healthy outdoor families and communities. More broadly it aspired to world unity. Paul later remembered the powerful effect of his Kibbo Kift years, noting that its practices had an 'other worldly appeal in a war-torn world'. In his 1946 book *The Living Hedge* he described a Kibbo Kift camp:

> The walls and roofs of tents were painted with camp-fires, Indian picture-writing, and symbolic green-clad figures, and beneath these canopies we sat in cross-legged quiet while a brilliantly robed procession of the chiefs beat the bounds of the camp and paused at each tent door to present us with the bodes – a carved oak leaf on an oak slab – to touch. When the full circle had been travelled, a herald in an embroidered robe quartered in scarlet and silver came to the totem-pole and with a loud cry summoned us to the Council Circle. Clad in jerkins and cowls of many colours, and mostly of a homely and an ill-fitting simplicity, we gathered in an uneven circle for the lighting of the fire which had not to be let die until our festival was ended.

The magical and mystical appeal of Kibbo Kift in the early 1920s, however, co-existed with a growing sense of dissatisfaction among

Kibbo Kift painted tent. The style, representing a family, is both folky and Cubist, 1928

An all-ages group of Kibbo Kift Kinsfolk with personally-made totems, c.1924. The similarity to early Woodcraft Folk costume in particular the placement of a badge on the left breast is striking (page 138)

some members about how the group was run. Hargrave's leadership was autocratic and he frequently made decisions about membership and policy without consultation and with no means of redress. For the democrats of the group, this dictatorial method betrayed the socialist promise they saw in the group's founding aims.

In 1924, after attempts to resolve the situation directly, a group of 32 dissenters compiled a circular leaflet to support the motion 'That the administration of Kibbo Kift during recent months has been profoundly unsatisfactory'. The signatories were led by Gordon 'Shada' Ellis, a teacher from South London working for the Royal Arsenal Co-operative Society and Joseph 'Silvertongue' Reeves, the author of regular Kibbo Kift articles in the co-operative magazine, *Comradeship and Wheatsheaf*. Significantly, it included three of the seven members who had been present at the inauguration of Kibbo Kift's covenant, along with Shaw and Paul. The leaflet listed a range of shortcomings and concluded with a vote of no confidence in Hargrave. At the 1924 Althing (Kibbo Kift's AGM), however, the co-operators were voted down by 88 to 55. Those who had lost the vote immediately walked out of the camp circle and out of Kibbo Kift.

As Paul would reflect in his 1977 autobiography, he and Shaw 'could not bear that all this picturesque and significant life-style should collapse and come to nothing.' So in 1925 the two gathered together a humble group of four boys in the hope of starting a new camping fellowship; to this they soon added girls and a developing political philosophy. As the groups grew, many aspects of Kibbo Kift's cultural methods were reproduced in the early Woodcraft Folk; many of these in turn had come from the inspiration of Ernest Thompson Seton, who had adapted Native American styles and systems of organisations for his earlier experiments in woodcraft training for youth in America. These ranged from the primitivist practices of totem poles, tom-tom

John Hargrave in his White Fox mask at children's 'Tribal Training' camp, 1928

Gleemen and Gleemen
(Kibbo Kift singers and
performers), 1929

drumming and dancing, to the use of animal or plant names for members, camp ceremonial circles and a mystical belief in the transformative power of nature and physical exercise. The emerging Woodcraft Folk policy also emphasised co-operative principles and had a clear central purpose: to develop the cultural, social and political education of workers' children.

As the first leader, or 'Headman', Paul's impressive talents shaped the Folk in distinctive ways as a democratic organisation, but as a very young person with little experience of youth group membership beyond Kibbo Kift, inevitably many of their influences were transposed wholesale into early Woodcraft Folk. For those that doubted their place in a movement focused on developing children as socialist citizens, Paul explained in 1936, 'The working class movement is deadly dull… It is our job to brighten it up and make it more attractive. Special emphasis therefore should be placed upon crafts which have a social value and which express some vital folk message'. This vital message was uncompromising from the outset and arguably reflected the utopian ambitions of Kibbo Kift. In 1926, despite their tiny numbers and limited means, Paul declared, 'We are the revolution. With the health that is ours and with the intellect and physique that will be the heritage of those we train, we are paving the way for that reorganisation of the economic system which will mark the rebirth of the human race.'

Three young
Woodcraft Folk
members out hiking.
The original caption
read 'Kinswomen
camping bent', 1930s

'We are training children for a new world'

Leslie Paul in
*The Republic of
Children*, 1939

Everything under the sun

A pacifist who enlisted; an atheist who found God. Who was Leslie 'Little Otter' Paul, the charismatic but contradictory co-founder of Woodcraft Folk?

Kit Jones

Leslie Allen Paul is a fascinating and perplexing figure. He spent his youth and twenties promoting a politics that was at once socialist, pacifist and saw religion as irrational. Then, as he reached his thirties, a combination of global and personal crises turned his world upside down.

This outspoken pacifist willingly signed up as a soldier in WWII and this ardent materialist found Christianity could help make sense of the war when his Marxism could not. So total was Paul's conversion he joined the Church of England and became a leading figure lecturing in theology.

The original angry
young man, Leslie Paul

Born in 1905, Paul grew up in a lower-middle class family in Whitechapel where his first job was helping his father sell newspaper advertising space. As a child he took every opportunity to escape into the countryside, with the Scouts, alone and through literature, spending whatever he earned from his father on either books or train tickets. His childhood was cut short by WWI, and his experience volunteering in a military hospital aged 12 stayed with him into adulthood.

When in 1920 John Hargrave, head of camping and woodcraft at the Scouts Association, left to set up the Kindred of the Kibbo Kift (page 14) Paul followed. Hargrave and Paul both felt that Scouts had retained a militarism and jingoism that didn't sit well in the wake of the war. They wanted Scouts to be a worldwide movement for peace and aged 16, Paul set up The Brockley Thing, a network of Kibbo Kift groups in south London, which was supported by socialists and co-operators. He also became the editor of *The Open Road*, an independent newspaper on scouting. When in 1924 a rift opened within Kibbo Kift over whether it should become democratic, Paul co-founded Woodcraft Folk with Sidney Shaw, drawing on his existing network across various British youth movements.

The young Paul now stamped his enormous character on Woodcraft Folk, in a remarkably enduring way. He was a socialist, perhaps even a communist at times, and during the 1926 General Strike, just as his early Woodcraft Folk groups were getting off the ground, Paul formed a 'council of action' to help organise the strikers in Lewisham and Deptford. (His account sounds much like my own experiences organising at a large camp: co-ordinating volunteers, printing publicity, collecting donations and distributing food.) When the strike defeated, Paul felt betrayed by the union leaders who had capitulated to the government rather then letting the strike escalate towards revolution. He joined and established many other left wing groups in the years preceding WWII including a Marxist discussion group, a committee on the nationalisation of coal

Leslie Paul as a boy in his Scouts uniform

mines with GK Chesterton, and in the mid-1930s, the Federation of Progressive Societies and Individuals – started by HG Wells and aiming to unite the left. Paul even edited its journal, titled *Plan*. But as his experiences in Scouts and Kibbo Kift show, he wasn't the kind of person whose politics would fit neatly into existing movements. He wanted Woodcraft Folk to be an institution of the left, and fought hard for recognition and support from co-operatives and other working class organisations. Yet writing in his 1951 autobiography *Angry Young Man* he also rebelled against 'the dreary working class movements with their endless committees and conferences meeting in dusty, smoke-laden halls, and lacking in colour, excitement and grandeur.'

In the early years of Woodcraft Folk there was a second movement, separate from socialism, that the organisation felt an affinity to:

> In our first contacts with such movements as the Kronacher Wandervogel and the Deutsche Freischar in the twenties we felt no doubt at all that we stood for the same things. We felt drawn to them much more than our own British Trade Union and Labour Movements. We had the same independence, the same love of the open air, the same eagerness to discuss everything under the sun. But now they were saying such dubious things that I was driven to look instead to international socialist contacts: for we were losing our first and best friends.

'Free' German Youth movements like those Paul mentions were largely self-organised by young people and thrived in Germany, in different guises, both before and after WWI. In the mid-1920s, when Woodcraft Folk was in contact with them, there were approximately 50,000 members of the various *Bündische* groups. What they had in common with Woodcraft Folk was a rebellion against modernity and a love of nature, as well as a reverence for a strong and fit body. Paul also says that the 'folk' in Woodcraft Folk was meant 'in the German sense of volk and not in the

English "fairy" or "arts-and-crafty" sense. It evokes a connection to an older, pre-industrial civilisation and connection with the land. As Hitler's rise began, Paul felt comforted by his Marxism that the 'menacing crank' would not get far in Germany – the country with 'the most powerful and best organised working class movement in the world... To this movement belonged history.'

Then in 1934 Paul had a breakdown. In just a few years his two fundamental belief structures had been crushed by the Nazis – the European youth movements in which he had seen freedom and idealism had either been outlawed or co-opted into Hitler Youth while the supposedly mighty organised working class had been divided and castrated. A trip to the USSR in 1931 compounded Paul's disillusionment with Marxism though it took some time to come to terms with it. He eventually came to publicly regret a report he wrote of his trip at the time which he later felt downplayed or excused the poverty and desperation he encountered.

The shock of global crisis was matched by personal crisis – the death of his father, following a period of alcoholism. Paul had been getting a lot of writing work through his father, whose business was doing well and had been living at home (the original millennial). He had, up until then, been able to plough much of his energy into Woodcraft Folk, but with virtually no savings he was financial ruined, with his Mother now relying on him for support. He was also in poor health, which, ironically, he attributed to years of outdoor life. In 1934 he resigned from active leadership of Woodcraft Folk, though he remained involved and honorary president, and fell into depression.

After several months in bed, barely surviving, he was rescued by a job teaching unemployed men, principally at Trinity, a church led by a radical clergyman called Reverend William Dick in Poplar. Trinity had a food bank, a night shelter, provided clothing and organised many clubs, meetings and classes. Paul's first lecture, on his experience in Soviet Russia, was not as we might imagine a small church-hall talk; there were several hundred

A portrait of Leslie Paul drawn by 'Anoki' in Tooting Woodcraft Folk's log book, 1927

braying and argumentative men – communists, anarchists and fascists among them. This job gave him a degree of financial stability for seven years until the outbreak of war.

His work as a writer led to critical acclaim and some notoriety, but not a great deal of income. He was devastated when his 1932 first novel, *Fugitive Mornings*, received rave reviews but then failed to sell more than a handful of copies. As well as novels, he published poems, essays and books on woodcraft. He also interviewed many prominent public figures including Bertrand Russell, GM Trevelyan and HG Wells. In one such interview Wells described the history taught in schools to him as the 'elaborate bloodstained twaddle of kings' a phrase that went viral across the international press. Another of Paul's phrases that still echoes through our lexicon is *Angry Young Man*, which was appropriated by a group of playwrights and novelists including Kingsley Amis, John Osborne and Alan Sillitoe and is still used to colour a particular kind of a young, frustrated politically-engaged activist of the left.

In 1938, Paul visited Prague and Vienna with the aim of establishing links to supply solidarity support from England for underground socialists in Austria and Germany. He planned to arrange English couriers regularly travelling between

Leslie Paul published many books in his career including *Angry Young Man* and *The Republic of Children*

Leslie Paul address a circle of young Woodcraft Folk members at a camp

Austria and England, carrying news and useful documentation. In the end his return trip home was the only one of these missions that occurred, as growing expectations of war made the vision impossible to realise. However he nonetheless brought back passports for several members who were about to slip into Switzerland. Paul traveled to Austria again in 1939, to camp with nearly 1000 Woodcraft Folk members which he described as 'a demonstration of European youth for peace and against fascism (not yet understanding that they could have one policy or the other, but not both together)'.

As the war reached London Paul experienced the full force of the Blitz. One night the road outside his flat was turned to a crater as he waited in a shelter with families from the other flats. He was called up to the army in 1941 and went to fight willingly, choosing not to join the conscientious objectors who were citing Woodcraft Folk membership in their trials. Woodcraft Folk reacted by removing him from his role as lifetime honorary president. Although he became a soldier he never fought on the front line. After completing his training he was posted to the Army Educational Corps, because of his experience in Poplar where he lectured on the causes of the war and contemporary affairs. He was relatively comfortable and had time on his hands to take up playing the flute, and spend a lot of time thinking about what he was going to believe in next now he was no longer a pacifist and felt Marxism inadequate. He puzzled about why he had felt compelled to fight the Nazis and realised it was more about a basic sense of morality than political conviction; that he found Christianity a good way to understand his impulse surprised him. He described the revelation as 'the rush of my own spirit towards a new freedom [that] was so rapid as to frighten me.' For Paul, fighting the Nazis took on a new meaning – as part of a larger spiritual conflict.

No longer connected to Woodcraft Folk or many of his old left comrades, after the war he had to reinvent himself. Much of his autobiography is scathing about his earlier leftism. Christianity provided the new community he needed and he became the director of studies at Brasted Place Theological College. Later he became a lecturer in ethics and social studies at Queens College, Birmingham, and theology at the University of Birmingham. In 1964 he wrote an extremely influential report commissioned by the Church of England, into the deployment and payment of clergy. According to *The Spectator* magazine at the time Paul's report painted a picture of a church that was 'still largely designed for looking after a settled pastoral community, in which the "squarson" occupies his well-defined place on the ladder of society.' Paul made a series of recommendations to make the church a more effective and relevant force in the modern world – many of which were taken up.

Finally, in 1985, three months before his death and in an act of reconciliation, Paul gave a lecture on the early years of the Woodcraft Folk. In it he praised the tenacity of the organisation for continuing to survive and thrive where many similar organisations have failed. He ended: 'My concluding words: I salute you.'

LESLIE PAUL
1905 - 1985
Author and Founder of the Woodcraft Folk
Lived Here

This red plaque commemorating Leslie Paul hangs on the wall of his former house

Complete volume of *Herald of the Folk* belonging to Alf 'Ash' Wess, a leader based in Stratford, London. The issues are bound with boot laces. Note the illustration in which a boy makes his way from the industrial city to a forested camp

Herald of the Folk

One of the earliest Woodcraft Folk publications, *Herald of the Folk* began a long history of inventive and diverse newspapers produced locally and nationally by the organisation. These publications draw stories, articles and illustrations from members across the movement (pages 76, 80, 186). Like many of its successors, *Herald of the Folk* contained news, advice, literature and educational articles. The striking image opposite is the cover illustration from the first issue, published in March 1927. It shows an apparently naked young man gesturing towards the sun and the Woodcraft Folk symbol in front of a painted A-frame tent. The aesthetics suggest the influences of both Modernism and folk art. The issue was produced for a Woodcraft Folk stall at an exhibition organised by Royal Arsenal Co-operative Society but, though beautiful, it proved too costly to continue with such high production values.

HERALD OF THE FOLK

QUARTERLY REVIEW OF THE COOPERATIVE WOODCRAFT FELLOWSHIPS

6^D

MARCH, 1927

Cover Design by Tomahawk.   Articles by Reginald Stamp, F. C. Perry,
Friar Tuck, &c.   Message from Prof. Hall.   **6d.**

WIDEAWAKE SUPPLEMENT!
Sketches by Hollow Horn Bear, and Anoki.

The first issue of
Herald of the Folk,
cover design by
'Tomahawk'

Meetings held-at Waldron Road Schools on Fridays at 7 till 9 for all
-at the Wigwam on Mondays for girls: Tues: & Weds. for

Spread from Tooting
Woodcraft Folk's
log book, 1927

Log books

Many Woodcraft Folk groups kept detailed
log books as the official record of the group's
adventures. Often a log book would relate
to a paticular event such as an international
exchange with contributions from everyone on
the trip. Members were encouraged to treat
the production of the log as a craft in itself and
many of the early examples are beautiful objects,
illuminated like monastic texts and written using
deliberately theatrical language.

At nine o'clock a party of jubilant
Vagabonds, Rangers and Pathfinders
met at Tooting Broadway Tube Station
to go together to Victoria Station,
where these high-spirited crafters boarded
the Shoreham train. Away from the hub-hub
and bustle of the mighty heart, the train
wended its way carrying these young joyful
people into the 'Hop County' where the
refreshing country air assailed our nostrils.
We found to our dismay that the train
ended its journey at Bromley south where
for an interval of 15 minutes we abided our

Spread from Wembley
leader George Morris'
(page 94) log of an
international camp in
Liège, Belgium, 1939

ALWAYS A GOOD HELPING.

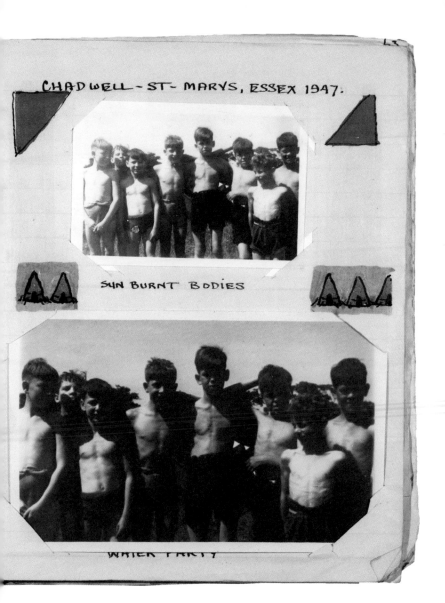

CHADWELL - ST - MARYS, ESSEX 1947.

SUN BURNT BODIES

WATER PARTY

Spread from a log
book entitled *Who's
for the Folk?*, 1947

Springbok the man of might.

Grey Fox at the cooking fire.

Austrian Red Falcons dancing with folk.

Bathing in the Wye. Brown Eagle at the back.

Plates up.!

Springbok of the supple limb.

Springbok the man of weight.

Red Spears Clan on Rota.

Springbok the ubiquitous.

Breakfast. Pine Top standing at back, left-centre.

Log Night 1947

Bottom: The log
book of Whitstun
Camp, May 1929

Top: Brighthelmstone
Thing log book.
Started 12 May 1937

the Thing visited the noble ruins of the Abbey & much did they marvel at their beauty & grandeur. It must be written that the guide who explained the abbey to us was himself a joy to all for he combined antiquarian lore with nautical humour and thus was unique amongst guides. From Tintern we journeyed on to a great cliff known as the Wyndcliff, from the top of which we saw a wondrous view across the Wye and the Severn, into the County of Gloucester and over many distant hills and rivers that we could not name. And albeit the rain prevented us from seeing the full glory of this view yet did we marvel at it. Then we went on to Chepstow another ancient town, where some of us visited the castle, but albeit a well preserved and doubtless interesting ruin there was no guide to shew us round and therefore its stones were dumb to us. Here in Chepstow we sat down to tea. It appeared to the Keeper of this Book that there were no bottoms to the stomachs of many of our Pioneers and greatly was he troubled at the thought of the Bill to come. Yet were there a few pieces left in the coffers of the Thing when the Bill was paid. After tea we continued through the Forest of Dean and the colliery town of Coleford back to the campsite. As we neared the campsite we came up with certain of the Clustanthing, led by Crown Eagle, who had hiked to the Speech House in the Forest. They boarded our last coach and returned to camp with us.

Visitors Day was the day of Saturn at the end of our first week. Many people from the countryside visited us together with some from Ross, Monmouth & other neighboring towns. It was on this day that the Folk sadly missed their Headman, Little Otter, whom sickness kept from the Camp. Hard as the camp leaders strove they could not wholly take his place. Yet must it be written that great work was done for the Folk on this day. Some Womfolk contracted a huge thirst in expounding to the strangers.

A contemporary Woodcraft Folk log book of Bromley Elfins' trip to Blackboys near the Ashdown Forest, August 2008

Photograph

A group of campers rest after a meal.
Note that one is sitting on a box of
Co-operative tea. Woodcraft Folk
has always sourced food for its camps
from co-operative businesses

Who are these folk all dressed in green?

Reflections on the first
fifty years of Woodcraft Folk
costume evolution

Annebella Pollen

The tituar question, posed in a 1935 article
introducing Woodcraft Folk, highlighted their
costumed character as a key distinguishing feature.
Their distinctive appearance singled the group out
among other youth, hiking and camping collectives
in the interwar years, and the original colour and
style can still be seen echoed in the badge-laden
dark green drill shirts and 'Woody Hoodies' worn
at local and national meetings today.

Early instructions prescribed a green jerkin
and shorts for boys and a leather-fringed frock
for girls; each needed a decorated or plaited
leather or raffia belt and a sheath for a camp
knife. Girls should add a coloured wimple
(headscarf) or leather headband. Importantly,
all elements had to be home-made. The word

Early green leather-fringed jerkin with decorative embroidered collar and sleeves and a hand-stitched belt

'woodcraft' is sometimes mistaken to mean the literal making of things out of natural materials, but here the message is correct: the importance of stepping outside of commercial culture was an essential part of early Woodcraft Folk ambitions; the hand-made 'livery of green' was intended to be anti-industrial.

The jerkin, usually laced at the neck with a leather thong and with leather fringing to resemble buckskin, shows the debt that early Woodcraft Folk owes to its core influences. Most immediately it references the style of the green-shirted Kibbo Kift (page 14), from whom many of Woodcraft Folk's founder members had split in 1924, but it also recalls the influence of

artist, author and naturalist Ernest Thompson Seton and his turn-of-the-century system of outdoor youth training, based upon romanticised aspects of Native American practices. All the woodcraft groups emerging in Britain after WWI adapted Seton's ideas to some extent, not least his ideal that there should be 'picturesqueness in everything', including dress.

The green costume was worn alongside ceremonial regalia donned by office-holders in early Woodcraft Folk camps; the Herald, for example, wore a blue and gold tabard with a cockerel to make announcements. At a fire-lighting ceremony, the Keeper of the Fire wore a red and black tabard with an emblazoned tree. In good weather, clothes were kept to a minimum; boys were encouraged to strip down to shorts. In his 1931 manual, *The Green Company*, Leslie Paul instructed members in no uncertain terms: 'You must sunbathe at camp' (page 144).

Costume was practical, but also symbolic. As well as levelling out social differences,

Above: Shorts were encouraged for sunbathing (screens were erected to protect girls' modesty). Below: A ceremonial Keeper of the Fire tabard

Early Woodcraft Folk shoulder tab. The red Blackletter embroidered font was later replaced with a Modernist san-serif style of lettering

it announced membership through sewn-on shoulder tabs, which declared Woodcraft Folk in embroidered Blackletter font. Its making and decoration demonstrated practical and artistic skills. Not only was the costume never 'uniform' in the military sense, it also lacked uniformity in practice. Early photographs and surviving examples show large scale customisation and individual creativity, from the styles and colours of the hand-stitched badges (page 138) to additional decoration on collars and cuffs. Folk names (page 50) were tooled and woven into belts, with allegiance to other organisations and campaigns shown through badges and the red neckerchiefs of the International Falcon Movement (page 70).

The importance of full and correct costume-wearing was repeatedly emphasised in early publications, where it was described as a duty of membership. The centrality of costume to the movement was especially highlighted in 1937. The Public Order Act outlawed the wearing of political uniforms in public meetings. Given Woodcraft Folk's explicitly anti-war and anti-fascist agenda, the movement faced and urgent need change their either costume or their constitution. The decision to change Woodcraft Folk policy – towards broader educational rather than political aims – rather than lose their characteristic green garb shows the fundamental significance of Woodcraft Folk's collective identity.

By the end of the 1940s the costume had straightened into a regulation green shirt and shorts with an optional green beret. The off-the-shelf kit was part of increasing desire to shape the Folk into a respectable mass movement with all decorative, symbolic – and some might say cultish – elements eradicated. At twenty-five years old, the movement resolved 'that we would dress as becomes our age' and that the organisation

A young member is served food while dressed in a Woodcraft Folk lace-up jerkin

should not be 'a small sect, quaintly dressed'.
The editor of the Woodcraft Folk magazine of
the day, *The Helper*, reflected in 1950, 'Maybe
it was the explosion of the atom bomb that woke
us to the fact that... our dress matters little
compared to our work'. Yet the costume firmly
remained, and its maintenance was still seen as
important. Wearers were instructed by Basil
Rawson in *The Woodcraft Way* in 1952: 'Keep your
costume neat and clean so neither your name
nor the name of the movement will suffer.'

The debates over Woodcraft Folk costume,
which have rumbled across the decades, have
tended to reflect wider campaigns to modernise,
recommended by those who, for example, also
seek to eradicate 'folk names' (page 50) and camp
ceremonies. These issues arise periodically and
tend to split along lines of those who find such

elements archaic and alienating and those who argue that these aspects give the movement its distinctive atmosphere. The debate about why and how costume should be worn also reflects wider discussion about co-operation versus individual preference. The challenge to a neat group appearance by the youth movement of the 1960s saw this played out in practice. A resolution in 1967 to impose a more definitive 'uniform' that was 'not subject to the extreme fluctuations of fashion' included efforts to regulate a respectable length for girls' skirts and reveals conflict between Woodcraft Folk's collective tradition and young people's increasing desire for autonomy and freedom of expression.

Photographs of Woodcraft Folk gatherings over time show the infiltration of elements of fashion into costume despite attempts at regulation. Green shirts are a constant, but they are also constantly adapted, whether through Peter Pan collars and puffed sleeves in the 1930s, for example, or the accompaniment of sunglasses and flares in the 1970s. Woodcraft Folk practices are mobile and just as the educational ethos has bent and flexed over time, so too have the ways by which they fashion a new world.

Watford Pioneers dancing in a circle, 1966. Their matching green drill shirts are typical of Woodcraft Folk's post-war costume

FOLK COSTUME
FOR WOMEN AND GIRLS 'RIVERINA
GREEN BLOUSE OR SHIRT, and
GREY, GREEN OR BROWN SKIRT
(SYMBOLS etc as BOYS.)

A Woodcraft Folk
logbook illustrating
costume advice, 1947

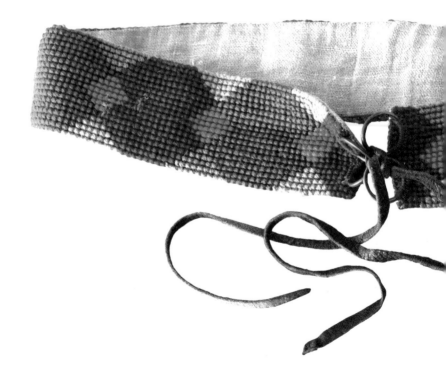

Belts
Early members made
their own belts. The
top example features a
Woodcraft Folk emblem
carved into the leather

49

What's in a name?

The curious custom
of alternative language
in Woodcraft Folk

Annebella Pollen
Distinctive terminology for Woodcraft Folk
practices and so-called 'folk names' for
members has been a long-standing aspect of
the organisation's culture. Membership has been
collectively known as 'kinsfolk', local groupings
were named 'Things', and individual members
were restyled with names of plants, animals or
characters from literature. Reading back through
historical documents, pseudonyms such as 'Swift
Canoe' or 'White Webfoot' seem archaic for
members of a progressive organisation devoted to
important, on-the-ground campaigns to educate
for social change. Why was such language used,
and why – in some cases – does it endure today?

As with many early woodcraft practices,
the origins can be found in the ideas of

Early needlepoint belt,
in, featuring a folk name

Ernest Thompson Seton, or in the group that
immediately preceded Woodcraft Folk, the
Kindred of the Kibbo Kift (page 14). Kibbo Kift
played with language, mingling colloquialisms from
antiquarian dictionaries with Anglo-Saxon terms
and, like many internationally-minded groups,
were enthusiasts of the new world language of
Esperanto. Seton's training scheme for young
people borrowed many elements from his reading
of Native American culture, including terminology,
and he discussed the process of 'winning a name'
for members of his groups in his 1912 publication,
The Book of Woodcraft. He described woodcraft
names as 'honourable nicknames given in
recognition of some exploit or personal gift'.

Seton was himself known as 'Black Wolf' and
suggested that members might be awarded names

that signalled positive attributes (Eagle-Eye, for example). When a new name was to be taken, the person's given name should be written on a piece of birch bark and ceremonially burned in a fire. These practices continued into Kibbo Kift, accompanied by elaborate initiation ceremonies. Members tended to choose their own names, although recommendations were also given to avoid sentimentality and duplication (too many members, it seems, fancied themselves as wolves). These names were explicitly understood as 'totem' names, where the animal or plant or mythological figure chosen would be honoured as a personal guide. The practice of taking a name was usually accompanied by the carving of a symbolic totem which would be carried on processions and treated with some sanctity. These would have been the conditions under which Leslie 'Little Otter' Paul (page 22) and other founding members of the later Woodcraft Folk received their folk names. In Paul's 1931 manual for young people, *The Green Company*, he explains, 'I was called "Little Otter" because I could swim', just as 'somebody with ginger hair was called "Red Spear"'. Alternative names for members continued enthusiastically in the early years of Woodcraft Folk, where they were especially valued for the way they negated ageist formalities of the day such as calling adults 'Miss' and 'Sir', creating instead a sense of equality between adult and child.

As Woodcraft Folk grew and modernised, particularly after WWII, some elements of the traditional language were dropped (the annual Althing meeting, for example, became the Annual Delegate Conference while the the Head Man became General Secretary). An article in the internal magazine, *The Helper* (page 78) from 1951 nonetheless defended the use of ceremonies as a means of non-military organisation and a way of creating a sense of belonging. Folk names continued throughout these years, although the sources from which those names might be drawn became more diverse now including characters from fairy tales and even comic strips.

Kibbo Kift 'Chickadee' totem, c.1928

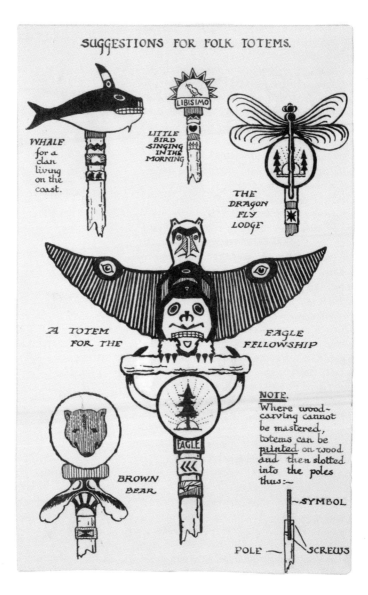

SUGGESTIONS FOR FOLK TOTEMS.

WHALE for a clan living on the coast.

LITTLE BIRD SINGING IN THE MORNING

LIBISIMO

THE DRAGON FLY LODGE

A TOTEM FOR THE

EAGLE FELLOWSHIP

EAGLE

BROWN BEAR

NOTE. Where wood-carving cannot be mastered, totems can be <u>painted</u> on wood and then slotted into the poles thus:—

~SYMBOL

POLE —

SCREWS

Early Woodcraft Folk carvings drew on various sources including First Nation and European folk traditions

Writing in the 1960s, Woodcraft Folk leader Basil 'Brown Eagle' Rawson acknowledged that the adoption of folk names 'is no longer as common ... amongst older age groups'. He noted, however, 'it should not be assumed that the growing pseudo-sophistication and more blasé attitudes of modern society have robbed [folk] names of their value to younger children.' Folk names, he argued, emphasised the special difference between group membership and life in the outside world, created bonds of affection, and added to the development of personal skills.

Rawson defended the use of naming ceremonies again in the early 1980s, when a heated dispute over the value of tradition in the organisation unfolded in the pages of *Woodcraft Focus* magazine. Rawson suggested, 'the ceremony was designed to impress the child with the idea that has was no longer a slave of "Mammon" or "the great god grind" but a rebel and one pledged to work for peace and friendship.' The changing make-up of the membership in the 1980s, however, led to a number of shifts that split the opinions of newer leaders and longer-standing members. Efforts to bring Woodcraft Folk into closer alignment with campaigns for anti-racism and anti-sexism meant that careful attention was paid to the wording of historic songs and creeds. Practices that were seen to be politically outmoded were uprooted or adapted. As recently as 2013 the Woodcraft Folk AGM passed a resolution to remove all gendered references from the national song book.

The use of folk language, however, has not died out completely. In camps today it is quite common to see members with folk names proudly embroidered into their Woody Hoodies or green drill shirts. In 2008 District Fellows (page 188) brought back 'Thing' as a term for their governance events alongside 'Althing', which they were already using to refer to their AGM. At the start of the 21st century a booklet of revised ceremonies was produced. In this updated version, the naming ceremony can be overseen by a 'Motemistress' as much as a 'Motemaster'.

Above: A wooden necklace made by Isabel 'Apple Belle' Cleveland shows her folk name on one side and given name on the reverse.
Right: 21st century staffs carved by Banbury members Phineas Harper and Christina Newman. These are not totems but show the continuing tradition of staff carving

55

Photograph
The Elfin clambering
over this gate is
Margaret 'Columbine'
White who grew up
to become General
Secretary and President
of Woodcraft Folk

Dress
A hand-made child's
Woodcraft Folk dress
with emblem badge,
shoulder tabs and
embroidered flowers

A cast lead version
of the Woodcraft Folk
emblem for printing

Venturer membership
card featuring the
imprint of the block

Printing blocks

Before digital technologies, printed materials were
produced using analogue processes to apply ink to
paper. For many years Woodcraft Folk produced
numerous printing blocks to make newsletters,
membership cards, publicity materials and posters.
Blocks were specially tooled from cast lead,
acid-etched or hand-carved from linoleum.

An original photograph
is acid-etched onto
a metal plate, which
is then attached to
a wooden block for
printing. The final
image is a mirror-image
on printing block

A triangular lino cut depicting the view of a smouldering camp fire through a tipi door

Linocuts

Acid-etching eventually allowed the cost-effective reproduction of photography in print but before then hand-made linoleum cuts were the primary way Woodcraft Folk publications were illustrated leading to a now lost tradition of linoleum art production across the organisation. Using sharp tools members would carve out small chunks of lino creating a negative of the final image. These thin lino pieces would then be mounted on blocks of wood to be fixed into trays called gallies with lead type letters for printing. Early publications such as *The Helper* (page 78) would use a specially-commissioned linocut as the cover page illustration for each issue.

The original printing
block and resulting
impression of a linocut
by 'Estrellita'

A striking linocut
from the May 1939
cover of Woodcraft
Folk periodical,
The Helper. Published
on the eve of WWII,
the image ran with
the caption 'Don't
die for Capitalism –
live for Socialism!'

This linocut was also published on a cover of *The Helper* a few months later as war broke out. Its depiction of a solitary peaceful camper suggests a sombre but stoic mood in the organisation

Story Without End
Leslie Paul's 1937 book, subtitled
The Junior Book of Co-operation,
features a silhouette that also appears
in the Woodcraft Folk archive, in
cruder form, as a hand-made linocut

STORY WITHOUT END

by
Leslie A. Paul

CO-OPERATIVE • UNION • LIMITED

Wembley Stadium.
A circle of Woodcraft
Folk tents surrounds
the central podium

International
Co-operative Day

On Saturday the 2nd of July 1938 London's
Wembley Stadium played host to a spectacular
choreographed celebration of co-operation and
co-operative organisations as part of an ultimately
unsuccessful campaign to promote international
peace. The show was like a modern day Olympic
opening ceremony with costumes, music, dancing
and large puppets telling multiple stories.
The strong bond between Woodcraft Folk and
the co-operative movement (page 134) was writ
large on the playing field when aproximately 500
Woodcraft Folk members took part, pitching a
vast circle of tents to show a co-operative camp
in front of an audience of 60,000.

Above: Linocut illustration from *The Helper* (page 78) showing the Co-operative Day celebrations.
Left: The official programme. Note the rainbow banner which was a of symbol of internationalism and peace (page 68)

Rainbow flag

Today the image of a rainbow is effectively synonymous with LGBT identity and pride campaigns but this is relatively recent. Woodcraft Folk and the wider co-operative movement have been using the rainbow as symbol of equality, internationalism and peace since the 1930s. Camps would fly rainbow flags alongside the bisected Woodcraft Folk flag (page 118) and members would regularly use rainbows to decorate stages, camps, literature and themselves.

A group of young Woodcraft Folk members raise a rainbow flag at a peace demonstration on the Isle of Wight, 1931

The central stage at the 1951 international camp in Debden, Essex was festooned with rainbow banners and flags

Badge from the 1988 Woodcraft Folk international camp

Banbury Pioneers hold out a rainbow peace flag at Global Village international camp, August 2006

Red bird of paradise

The story of the International
Falcon Movement – Socialist
Education International

IFM-SEI is a network of 50 children's organisations
across the world, of which Woodcraft Folk is
one. The network began in the 1920s with a
small group of continental working class socialist
organisations comparable to Woodcraft Folk
in many ways but with their own visual identity
and costume tradition of bright blue shirts
and red falcon emblems. By 1927 organisations
from Denmark, Latvia, Hungary, Switzerland,
France, Poland and Belgium had joined and an
international camp was held – the first 'Children's
Republic' at Seekamp in Germany.

WWII dealt a terrible blow to the fledgling
falcons, practically shutting it down for the
duration of hostilities until the critical 1946

Above: A Red Falcons shirt complete with iconic red neckerchief. Top Left: An enamel Red Falcon pin badge. Bottom Left: Earrings in the image of two young Red Falcons

international camp in Brighton (page 92) was able to jump-start the rebuilding process. Seven years later at a conference in Nuremberg the International Falcon Movement was officially founded. Later it expanded its name after a period of membership growth to accommodate Israeli, Palestinian, Indian and other organisations without a history of falcon symbolism.

By the 1990s IFM-SEI had expanded to Latin America and was organising campaigns that ranged from promoting reproductive health education to fighting child labour and sexual abuse. Through IFM-SEI Woodcraft Folk engages in EU and UN policy making while participating in a vast international youth network.

Brighton international camp, 1937

31 July 1937 marked the start of a three week international camp on the white cliffs of the South Downs near Brighton. The camp was the first Woodcraft Folk had a hosted of its scale or complexity, more than double the size of the previous Forest of Dean 'Mass Camp' in 1933. Reports from the camp proudly reveal that 2000 children from ten countries were fed with 40 imperial tons of food including 500 dozen eggs, all of it purchased through co-operatives.

The camp was provocatively international at a time of rising xenophobia. One night a group of Nazi sympathisers broke in to the site, stealing a flag from its pole. In response Woodcraft Folk organised night watchers to guard the flags – among them couple-to-be Joan 'Oakapple' and Sam 'Kingfisher' Pover, then 15 and 16, whose son, Martin served on the editorial board for this book. A large delegation of Czechoslovakians attended the camp making friendships which would later lead to Woodcraft Folk's instrumental role supporting the Kindertransport evacuating Jewish children from Nazi Europe (page 86).

Three girls from a European Red Falcon (page 70) group playing accordions while on the camp

Screen printed note
paper showing children
raising a red flag

A full-page illustration from *Hallo*, the camp newspaper, showing the various activities undertaken throughout the day from waking up to a sousaphone alarm clock at 7.30am until going to bed at 10pm

Camp organiser, Henry 'Koodoo' Fair, addresses campers in front of a large rainbow flag (page 68).
The camp was organised into villages of tents based on shared language. Leaders from all delegations met each night to evaluate the day's successes and to draft activities for the next day, distributing written programmes in English, German and French

Chorus of *Vagrant Song* published in *Hallo*, the camp newspaper

O ye comrades, O ye workers,
Forth unto the wild again,
And the city? What a pity.
Knock it down and build it sane!

THE PROCESSION

—see account on page 1

The Pioneer

The Pioneer of the Folk and later, *New Pioneer* were Woodcraft Folk periodicals that followed on from *Herald of the Folk* (page 30). The magazines were produced by a team of members who named themselves, jokingly, 'The Press Gang'. A report from 'Lone Wolf' in the 1934 Woodcraft Folk Year Book tells how the machinery used to duplicate pages required each sheet of paper to be fed and removed manually. With a circulation of 450 and 14 pages per issue this meant a huge amount of feeding, folding and stapling.

The Pioneer of the Folk, September-October 1934. The procession depicted in the cover linocut would have been something like the one on the dust jacket of this book

New Pioneer, August 1939. The cultural references emerging from the camp fire smoke range from Robin Hood and a United States lumberjack to a Viking

New Pioneer,
August 1936

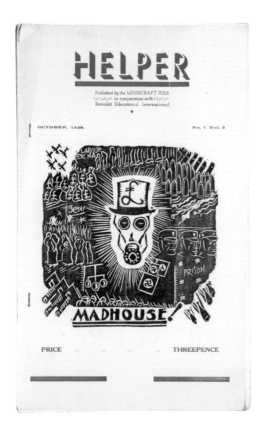

The Helper,
October 1938.
The illustration
simultaneously critiques
the rise of European
fascism and rampant
American corporatism
with the slogan
'Madhouse'

The Helper

This monthly magazine reveals a shift in
Woodcraft Folk's internationalism with its design
and writing. The bold, legible design would feature
a striking linocut print produced by a member and
resonating with issues of the day from upcoming
Woodcraft Folk activities to global politics. *The
Helper* was a vehicle for a prosaic ensemble of
announcements and messages to the membership
but it also provided a regular space for the
movement to collectively discuss and develop
its political response to Nazism through polemics,
reports and calls to action.

The Helper, June 1938.
This issue's front cover
was promoting the large
camp held the same the
summer of its publication

The Helper, April 1939.
The cover shows a girl
stepping from Dover to
Ostend leaving behind
the chimneys of the city

The Helper,
July-September 1942.
This wartime issue
reveals how Woodcraft
Folk was forced to cut
back on its activities.
Issues became text-only,
published quarterly
rather than monthly

Our artist's impression
of the New Forest where
Tooting, Enfield, Dagenham
Walthamstow and a number
of Swedish and German
Falcons are camping this
Summer.

Illustration from
The Helper, July
and August issue, 1953

Woodcraft Folk against the Nazis

Woodcraft Folk emerged from optimistic post-WWI utopianism. As the German Wiemar Republic gave way to autocratic Nazi rule it was a bitter realisation for the movement that another global conflict was looming. Despite the Nazi's nominal socialism, Woodcraft Folk leaders quickly realised that the 'National Socialists' were a brutal and authoritarian regime. While the British government embarked on a policy of appeasement, Woodcraft Folk publications were filled with condemnations of the Hitler Youth, concentration camps and antisemitism.

As international tensions escalated with the annexing of Austria and the Nazis closed down or took over Woodcraft Folk's sister organisations, members began raising funds to support those targeted by Nazi oppression. A plea in a 1934 issue of *The Pioneer* (page 76) declares, 'we must help them.' Later Woodcraft Folk members led by Henry Fair would be instrumental in supporting the Kindertransport which rescued many children from Czechoslovakia (page 86). Meanwhile members continued to organise large international children's camps in the United Kingdom and continental Europe, attempting to build peaceful coalitions among working class people across fraught borders.

During the war Woodcraft Folk members were deeply divided in their ethical response. Many of service age held staunch pacifist principals and became conscientious objectors, supported by the organisation. Others saw WWII as a morally-justified fight against fascism and enlisted or served as field medics, Leslie Paul among them (page 22). Neither side saw American capitalism and the inequality it created as a positive alternative. This led to the Woodcraft Folk declaring official neutrality throughout the war despite their loathing of Nazism.

A linocut published
on the cover of *The
Helper's* 1938 Christmas
issue, drawing attention
to Nazi death camps

They need our help!

In Austria friends of ours are going hungry or are in actual danger of imprisonment or death. It must seem like a terrible thing to you that the mothers or fathers of those brown and gay boys and girls who camped with you in the Wye Valley last year are now suffering from a persecution you cannot imagine. Because their parents were Socialists, members of their Labour Party, or Trade Unionists and Co-operators, or because their fathers and brothers fought and fell in defence of Austrian freedom, many children, many Red Falcons whom you have camped or corresponded with are now faced with want, even with actual starvation.

We can help them.

We must help them.

From a plea by 'Blue
Swift', published in
The Pioneer, 1934

This photograph
shows campers of five
nationalities as a rebuke
to rising racism in the
UK and Europe, 1934

Refugee crisis

The role Woodcraft Folk and
Henry 'Koodoo' Fair played in
the Kindertransport rescuing
children from Nazi persecution

Saskia Neibig

Against a backdrop of German expansionism, the
Spanish Civil War and a rise of fascism and racism
across the continent, Woodcraft Folk hosted
a Czechoslovakian delegation of 250 at the
Brighton international camp held at Rottingdean
in the summer of 1937 (page 72). This kind of
internationalism has always been common in
Woodcraft Folk but this particular camp resulted
in life-saving friendships. The Rote Falken, or 'Red
Falcons', were Czech teenagers of both Jewish
and non-Jewish heritage. They learned, played and
camped together like Woodcraft Folk did, but met
and spoke in German. Woodcraft Folk had already

HALLO !

NEWS PAPER OF THE INTERNATIO'NAL CHILDRENS' CAMP
LAGERZEITUNG DER INTERNATIONALEN FALKENREPUBLIK
JOURNAL DE LA REPUBLIQUE INTERNATIONALE DES FAUCONS ROUGES

BRIGHTON 1937

2000 children of eight different countries,
enfants de huit pays différents,
Kinder aus acht verschiedenen Ländern.

PUBLIE PAR L'INTERNATIONALE DE L'EDUCATION SOCIALISTE. DRAVEIL (S.-O.). FRANCE.

Front cover of the 1937 Brighton camp's newspaper. Note the Czechoslovakian delegation are shown carrying instruments - a nod to the 60-strong brass band they brought

provided a ready welcome in their membership to a young Austrian refugee called Susanna Medus, her family having fled Germany because of her father's left-wing journalism. Diaries from the time record that the Falcons who attended the camp in Brighton were surprised by the 'small mattresses' they ate for breakfast (Shredded Wheat) and the triangular sandwiches, without crusts, filled with 'grass' (mustard and cress). They also visited their counterparts in Antwerp to attend the 'Worker's Olympiad' and returned to Eastern Europe afterwards with memories and friendships, but thinking little more of it. Later in 1939 the Nazis were agitating in the

Sudetenland in western Czechoslovakia as the country prepared for invasion. Only five Falcon groups would remain inside the new border prompting Willi Hocke, the Brighton delegation leader, to send a friend, Vicki Schless, to London to ask for help. Woodcraft Folk's response was enthusiastic. Henry Fair, the national organiser at the time, wrote an impassioned letter to groups around the country. Hocke was arranging for hundreds of children to flee to Belgium with the help of those friends they had made there the previous summer. Fair asked for Woodcraft Folk groups to fundraise to support this operation. He exhorted them to encourage their children to send their pennies and argued that, despite Woodcraft Folk's own financial difficulties 'this is a period of sacrifice by workers for workers'. In 'solidarity with our Czech comrades', he suggested that refugees would soon need to come to England and asked that people volunteer to host children on a temporary basis. Monday was raised to send to Hocke and 40 homes were offered. Various bureaucratic obstacles delayed these offers: hosts needed to provide two references, promise to adopt the child until the age of 18, educate them and provide £50 (10% of the average annual income) as a guarantee to the authorities. Woodcraft Folk organised for at least 20 children to come and stay with their members and Woodcraft Folk groups also raised money to pay the guarantees for a few of them.

Susanna Pearson (neé Ehrmann) remembers boarding a train from Prague on the 29th June 1939 with 241 other children aged five to fifteen. At age 11 she did not realise at the time that she would never see her parents again. She was one of the last children to make it out safely and war broke out before all the offered homes could be filled. Arrival in England was not the end of the saga. Having co-ordinated the transport of the Falcons with Nicholas Winton, who brought 669 Czech children to the UK, Fair often had to maintain contact with the children's relatives who had escaped to the UK and those concerned parents left behind. He co-ordinateed

Henry Fair's letter to all of Woodcraft Folk, 1 November 1937

'Hundreds of the parents of Red Falcon members are in peril of their life, hundreds are refugees, sleeping in fields and ditches. Their children, ex-Red Falcons, many of them came to Brighton, are amongst these and they plead with their fellow comrades of other countries for help. Well what can we do, what can you ?'

Extract from
Henry Fair's letter

accomodation, bursaries and welfare of children with the Czech section of the Refugee Children's Movement. For many host families Woodcraft Folk was the only source of support. Testaments from Kindertransport survivors show that adjustment to their new life was not always easy. There were often cultural and language differences as well as the challenges of the war to overcome, but by taking Falcons into Woodcraft Folk homes the foster parents were able to provide an upbringing with a familiar value system and access to a sympathetic youth group. At first Pearson refused to leave Prague. She remembers being comforted by her parents who told her it would be 'like a

Falcon camp'. She remembers that the transition to life in Sheffield was hard While living with Basil Rawson, Headman of Woodcraft Folk, she had to learn English and live in an old fashioned semi-detached house that was a world apart from her apartment in Prague. Her education was disrupted by the outbreak of war because the school did not have an air raid shelter. She remembers hating the 'very odd food' like custard. The transition was made more bearable for those who attended Woodcraft Folk groups because camps which took place in Derbyshire and Epping Forest gave them familiar experiences. The friendships formed in these groups made it significantly easier to adjust to a new school environment.

In 1939 the Liege camp provided perfect cover for Henry Fair to smuggle two Czech boys into the UK in order to protect them from kidnapping by the Gestapo who wanted to intimidate their father. They had no passports but were hidden amongst the Woodcraft Folk delegation of 700 children. Fair ensured that they had already been living in London for seven months before he had to inform the government of their presence when the boys needed ration books. His efforts ensured their safe presence in the UK throughout the war and afterwards.

The Kindertransport was a huge operation, bringing 20,000 children from Germany and Nazi occupied countries to the UK. The British government was reluctant to take more and frequently obstructed the efforts of organisers. Most of the children of the Kindertransport found out after the war that their parents had been killed. Many remained in the UK to continue the lives they had built, with some emigrating to Israel, USA, South America and elsewhere. A few returned home to rebuild what remained of their communities. Many fai0th organisations at the time were engaged in similar work but Woodcraft Folk seems to have been the most significant secular organisation involved. Several Woodcraft Folk refugees stayed on in the UK and their children in turn went on to attend Woodcraft Folk groups and camps.

Front page of the *Western Daily Press*, 6 October 1995

Henry Fair is carried aloft by Woodcraft Folk members including Basil Rawson in his beret

In 1946, in the aftermath of a war and alongside new bread rations, Woodcraft Folk hosted another international camp again at Rottingdean (page 94), nine years after the first. There they united more than a thousand people from all over Europe to continue their unflinching internationalism. Decades later, at the age of 88, Henry Fair discovered that he had been placed on Hitler's hit list for his actions. He commented to the *Western Daily Press,* which ran the story with other newspapers, 'I felt a sensation of shock on learning that I was a target. But on reflection, I consider it to be something of an honour to have been wanted by the Gestapo.'

Cover design from the programme of the 1946 international camp

Brighton international camp, 1946

With WWII underway, Woodcraft Folk began making ambitious plans for an international camp which would bring together countries from war-torn Europe. At the time many considered the plan unthinkable. In the end the camp took place in Brighton and was a pivotal moment for international youth work, laying the foundations for many subsequent events. It sent a powerful and positive message: less than a year after the horrors of the war, young people from previously fighting nations were living and playing alongside each other in friendship and peace. It was a controversial move and suffered some negative press attention including widespread, but entirely false, reports of 700 tents blowing down in storms.

The *Brighton and Hove Herald*, which reported on the camp. The local mayor was impressed and is quoted saying, 'I feel sure that the best way to ensure world peace is to make it possible for children of different countries to exchange visits.'

A tug of war (or tug of peace?) adjudicated by Basil Rawson

The story of George Morris

In researching this book, the editors pieced together a tale of international friendship cut short by war

Jonny Helm

It's a shock to read the letter that Woodcraft Folk leader George Morris received in 1950. A simple translation from the French leaves space enough for the reader to fill with their own horrifying detail. The correspondence notes: 'We have had, like you, a very bad war.' Abruptly we hear of the fate of George's friend, Coussaint Frenay, 'dead in a concentration camp'. This news arrived with George a decade after he first met Frenay on the eve of WWII. With the letter are two calling cards; one from Frenay himself, a local policeman, and the other from Bertrand Fanson, who we assume is the letter's author. Both cards are from addresses in Wandre, Liège in Belgium

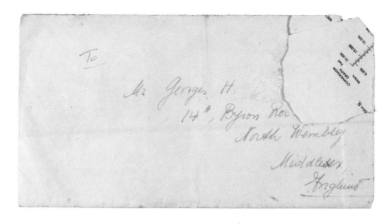

This envelope carried the letter to George with sad news of Coussaint's death in a concentration camp. It is made from old maps and addressed to North Wembley, where George was a Woodcraft Folk leader

where, in August 1939, Woodcraft Folk sent a delegaton to join a large international camp.

The camp followed on from the success of the 1937 international camp in Brighton (page 72). 700 Woodcraft Folk members are thought to have gone to the camp which was co-ordinated by Henry Fair, who was at the time organising shelter for Czechoslovakian refugee children from the Red Falcon Movement (page 70). Return tickets to Dover on chartered trains and on the Princess Marie Jose steamer from Dover to Ostend were all included in the event ticket price. Morris was at the camp and returned with a set of photographs and memorabilia collected in his log book. We don't know how he met Bertrand

and Frenay but know their friendship was vividly remembered 11 years later.

The camp coincided with the anniversary of the declaration of WWI and all 1,300 campers visited the vast military cemeteries. Two days before a camp-wide peace festival a group of young people travelled by boat along the new Albert canal, a key part of Belgium's former defences against German invasion. The camp concluded on 12 August just three weeks ahead of Britain's declaration of WWII.

We can't find records of Morris during the war years but his story surfaces again in 1945 as he registers three groups, the Pinedwellers, Treetops and Hillrangers, from the same North Wembley address that the letter reached in 1950.

YOUNG WOODCRAFT FOLK at the International Children's Camp at Wandre, Liege, Belgium.

A spread from George's log book recording his trip to Wandre with photos, postcards and linocuts from the camp. Left: The train ticket was specially printed by Southern Railway as Woodcraft Folk had charted a whole train for the journey

Morris has written on Bertrand's card 'two photos', either a reminder or an errand recalled later. Between the camera exposure and the prints' delivery the war took over 60 million lives. Bertrand's additional note translates: 'I'm sending back a photo to the family of Frenay who send you all their thanks for the beautiful memory. Thinking of Wandre again with much affection.'

George Morris is not unique in forging international friendships. Connections between people are made by individuals not their organisations, but the organisation is the platform on which they are built. His is one of many inspiring stories which we hope may be looked on in another 90 years with the same amazement the editors of this book felt while uncovering it.

Play, politics and parachutes

The strategic deployment of paratroopers in World War II required the production of silk parachutes in unprecedented numbers. After the war, the army sold off the redundant pieces of equipment for a fraction of their production cost. Despite their tainted history, parachutes proved to be cheap and brilliant tools for Woodcraft Folk play, giving rise to enduringly popular parachute games. Old parachutes are of little use to an individual but, when held by a group, enable collective activities making them ideal for exploring co-operative values in fun and varied ways. Local groups snapped up ex-military parachutes and later would even make their own 0in rainbow or Woodcraft Folk colours.

In time parachutes proved themselves to have another function as objects of political protest. Mass demonstrations are tough places for children and adults alike – often slow-moving, crowded and long. Using a parachute on a protest not only provides a colourful activity that can move with the procession but also creates a small clearing in the crowd, guaranteeing an area of refreshing open space. Like trade union banners and witty placards, the Woodcraft Folk parachute has become a regular sight at protests, subverting its roots in the establishment war machine.

Woodcraft Folk groups
play parachute games
outside the Houses of
Parliament to protest
youth work cuts, 2008

Parachute games
on camp, 1980s

Woodcraft Folk
children dash under the
billowing dome of a
parachute 'mushroom'

A parachute creates a space for games at the Refugees Welcome march through London, 12 September 2015

A Woodcraft Folk group huddles under a parachute held taut by sitting on its edges

Skirt

From 1940 to 1970. Woodcraft Folk member Gladys 'Silver Birch' Brooker decorated this skirt made from recycled blackout material that had previously been used to cover windows during bombing raids in WWII. She stitched badges on the skirt from every country she visited and embroidered the word 'friendship' in many different languages. The skirt was given to the Woodcraft Folk after Gladys died in 2003 aged 93

Medal and Banner

This hand-made hanging banner and brass medal commemorate a huge international camp held in Vienna in 1958. In both objects, the Woodcraft Folk emblem can be seen alongside the red birds of the International Falcon Movement (page 70)

A young teenager
presents their cleaned
tent at a camp in
Haselmere, 1938

Wapenshaw

Vápn schaw is an old Norse expression meaning
'weapon show'. In some military contexts, the
Anglicised 'wapenshaw' is still used to describe
a regular inspection of equipment including
firearms. Wapenshaw was used by Kibbo Kift
(page 14) to mean a display of crafted items. Early
Woodcraft Folk camps appropriated the term
for a practical ceremony in which each camper
removes all belongings from their tent and lays
them out. This serves to air out the tent, and to
ensure that no items have been lost. For some
Woodcraft Folk groups wapenshaw is about
symbolically demonstrating that pacifist campers
have no weapons in their equipment.

Carol Baxter does
Wapenshaw at camp
in Epping Forest, 1979

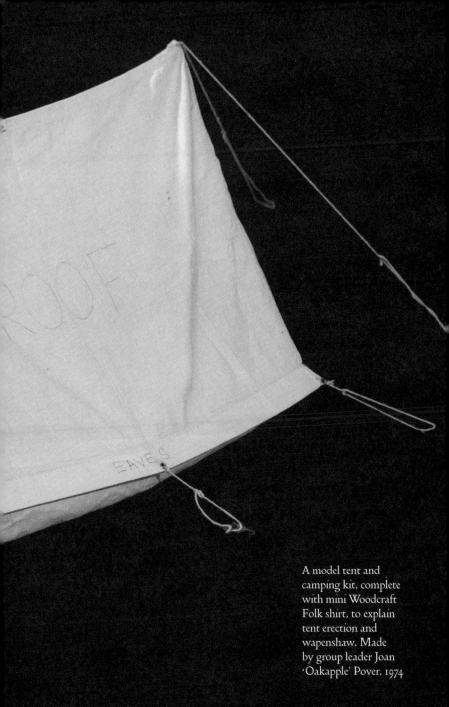

ROOF

EAVES

A model tent and camping kit, complete with mini Woodcraft Folk shirt, to explain tent erection and wapenshaw. Made by group leader Joan 'Oakapple' Pover, 1974

Wildwood Gadgets

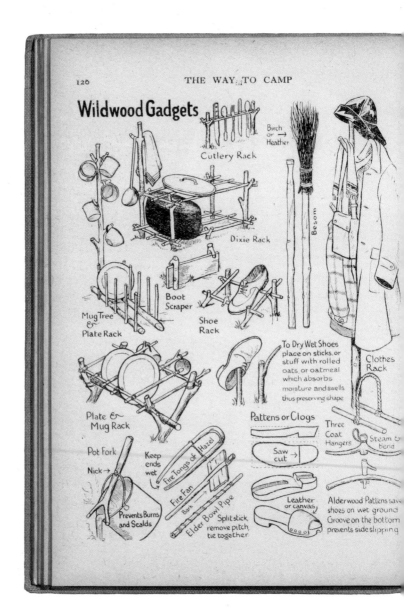

Cutlery Rack

Birch or Heather →

Besom

Dixie Rack

Mug Tree & Plate Rack

Boot Scraper

Shoe Rack

To Dry Wet Shoes place on sticks, or stuff with rolled oats, or oatmeal which absorbs moisture and swells thus preserving shape

Clothes Rack

Plate & Mug Rack

Pattens or Clogs

Three Coat Hangers

Saw cut →

Steam & bend

Pot Fork

Nick →

Keep ends wet

Fire Tongs of Hazel

Fire Fan

Bark

Elder Bowl Pipe

Split stick, remove pitch, tie together

Prevents Burns and Scalds

Leather or canvas

Alderwood Pattens save shoes on wet ground. Groove on the bottom prevents side slipping

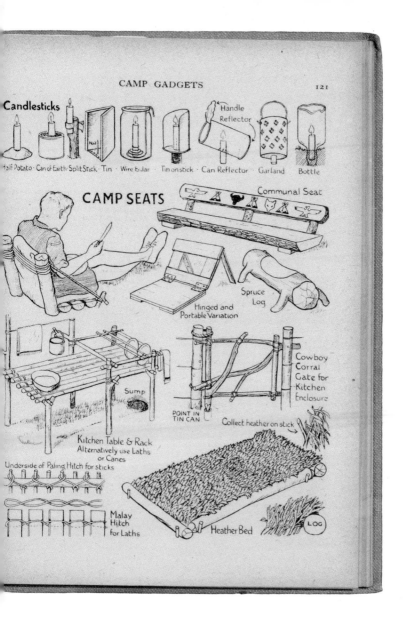

Candlesticks

Half Potato · Can of Earth · Split Stick · Tin · Wire & Jar · Tin on stick · Can Reflector · Garland · Bottle

Handle
Reflector

CAMP SEATS

Communal Seat

Hinged and Portable Variation

Spruce Log

Cowboy Corral Gate for Kitchen Enclosure

POINT IN TIN CAN

Sump

Kitchen Table & Rack
Alternatively use Laths or Canes

Underside of Paling Hitch for sticks

Malay Hitch for Laths

Collect heather on stick

Heather Bed

LOG

DIY gadgets from
Woodcraft Folk member
S. H. Walker's 1946 book
The Way to Camp

III

Singing

Songs have played a key role in reflecting and
developing the character of Woodcraft Folk's
values. From the early years, official songbooks
have been filled with a mix of whimsical ditties,
odes to the natural world and highly political
protest chants. The exact repertoire of songs that
each group knows varies by region so visitors to a
large camp might hear some members belting out
civil rights anthem *Back of the Bus* and different
groups singing the traditional folk song *Stewball
the Drunken Horse* at the same campfire.

A mixed international
choir singing together

Left and below:
The Ashen Stave,
an early book of songs
by Leslie Paul (page 22)

Watford, Harrow and
Wealdstone districts
sing together around
a pagoda fire, c.1965

The second edition
of *Songs for Venturers*,
a pocket book of
songs intended for
13-15 year olds. An
accompanying cassette
tape was produced with
recordings of the first
verse and chorus of
every song in the book

A seven inch vinyl of Waltham Forest Woodcraft Folk's version of *Imagine* by John Lennon

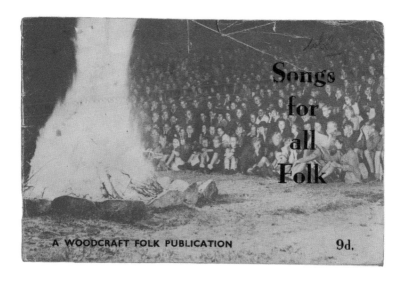

Songs for all Folk, a book of songs intended for all ages

The redesigned
Campfire Songs
for Woodcraft Folk
pocketbook, 2014

Link Your Hands Together

Link your hands together a circle we'll make;
This bond of our friendship no power can break.
Let's all sing together in one mighty throng;
Should any be weary we'll help them along;

Let us then laugh lightly if sadness should fall,
May joyous laughter spring from us all,
Helping each other we'll lighten the load,
Arms linked with comrades we travel the road.

Let us march together with firm step and strong,
As out from the darkness we all go along,
All sorrow is banished we march to the light,
Link your hands together, we're strong in our might.

One mighty throng

Link Your Hands Together has been popular
across Woodcraft Folk groups for decades. It
is traditionally sung at the end of meetings and
camps with participants holding hands in a circle
as they sing the first verse. It is unequivocally
a song about power - both in the sense of the
strong supporting the weak and of the collective
strength that comes from co-operative action.
Strikingly, the words of verses two and three
paint a picture of a march or political protest
where friendship and laughter is the bedrock
of a mighty procession. The song was originally
translated from the German version *Kommt Reicht
Eurer Hander* by Hannes Marzen and was first
picked up by Woodcraft folk at a 1927 socialist
children's camp at Seekamp in Germany.

Link your hands together
a circle we'll make
This bond of our friendship
no power can break

Let's all sing together in one mighty throng
Should any be weary we'll help them along

Let us then laugh lightly if sadness should fall
May joyous laughter spring from us all
Helping each other we'll lighten the load
Arms linked with comrades, we travel the road

Let us march together with firm step and strong
As out from the darkness we all go along
All sorrow is banished we march to the light
Link your hands together, we're strong in our might

By Hannes Marzen

Woodcraft Folk flag

The green and red flag

Woodcraft Folk's bisected flag has been in use since the begingings of the movement. It shows a red and green rectangle divided diagonally into two triangles, often with Woodcraft Folk symbol in the top corner of the green segment.

The flag symbolises the combination of socialist and envrionmentalist ideas that underpin Woodcraft Folk values and it forms part of a wider history of protest flags. The famous red and black anarchist flag, first used by the Spanish anacho-syndicalist movement Confederación Nacional del Trabajo (founded in 1910) has a strikingly similar design but with anarchist black instead of green. Subsequent activist movements have adapted the bisected flag to their ideologies with their own two-colour combinations, such as the pink and black of queer anarchism, the purple and black of anarcho-feminism, or the orange and black of mutualism.

The Woodcraft Folk
flag and a rainbow
flag (page 68) flying
in Finsbury Park,
London, 1995

Woodcraft Folk flag
in a camp circle, 1970s

The Mossback Lodge was an early group whose members included Leslie Paul and his brother, 'White Webfoot'. Speed the Plough is a traditional saying, popular in folk ballads, that indicates encouragement. The Mossback logbook of 1926 declares, 'Speed the Plough of Woodcraft!'

Banners

Banners have been a key part of Woodcraft Folk's campaign materials since its inception. Colourful handmade textiles hang on walls at club nights and declare group identity in text and image at galas and fetes, processions and protests. The styles of Woodcraft Folk banners have changed over time – from the highly skilled silk needlework, fringes and tassels of the early days to the felt, fabric paint and collectively-executed designs of more recent years – but shared motifs remain. Whether waved in support of the General Strike in 1926, the Festival of Britain in 1951 or demonstrations against student fees in the 2000s these banners share a stylistic solidarity with the campaign textiles of the trade unions, suffragettes and the co-operative movement, on whose shoulders Woodcraft Folk stand.

THE WOODCRAFT FOLK

MARSHLANDERS
FELLOWSHIP

Shield shape banners
have their origin in the
heraldic stylings of 19th
century friendly societies
and co-operative guilds.
The Marshlanders'
imagery shows the
importance of nature
to Woodcraft Folk

The term 'thing'
comes from an
Icelandic word for a
political assembly. It
was in use throughout
Kibbo Kift and early
Woodcraft Folk and is
still used by the District
Fellows (page 188)

Early Woodcraft Folk saw camping and hiking as nomadic in spirit. In 1932, 'Blue Swift' wrote, 'The people of a more advanced world will be civilised nomads, getting all the advantages of both the wandering and settled lives'

Woodcraft Folk groups frequently described themselves as Fellowships, echoing William Morris's socialist dictum: 'Fellowship is Life'

Ealing District's 2015 banner shows the enduring symbolism of camping as an antidote to urban industrialisation

The London region banner held aloft at the TUC-organised Future That Works march, 20 October 2012

Woodcraft Folk
members with willow
and paper lanterns
participate in solstice
celebrations in
Brighton, 2015

This banner features the
symbol and slogans of
co-operative education

Dancing Trophy
Despite a broadly non-competitive pedagogy, certain Woodcraft Folk groups used to compete in activities. This trophy for dancing was first awarded in 1953 to the Wayfarers Elfin group

Photograph
A meal is served in the first Woodcraft Folk national office, a stable loft in Balham, south west London, c.1934

Sign
The wooden sign which hung outside Woodcraft Folk's former office at 13 Ritherdon Road. A report in the July 1939 issue of *The Helper* reported: 'The letters are part of the back and not applied separately. The plate is stained in light and dark oak, thus making the actual name stand out. This fine piece of work was done by Keek of Stafford who has already some fine totems to his credit'

Power in a union

On the organised
labour movement
and Woodcraft Folk

Paul Bemrose
Woodcraft Folk is the only youth organisation
that states in its constitution that every adult
and young person moving into the field of work
should join an appropriate trade union. There is
simply no other youth movement that recognises
the deep importance of organised labour to such
a degree. The wider labour movement has always
been interested in the education of the young,
in part to create the next generation of activists
and to sow the seeds of change required for
value shifts in wider society. The co-operative
movement was perhaps more advanced than
most in this regard, supporting Woodcraft Folk
and running comparable youth organisations
from the early 20th century.

Trade unions tended to be slower and
more conservative. Perhaps because they have
traditionally been narrowly focused on winning

An advert for the Labour Party which ran in the first issue of Woodcraft Folk's periodical *Herald of the Folk* (page 30)

immediate improvements to workers' conditions, they have often directed resources to the here and now rather than looking to the future. This is not to say that individuals and groups of trade unionists didn't see the importance of youth. To an extent the problem wasn't necessarily that trade unions didn't want young members, it was rather the expectation that the world of work would create the conditions where young people automatically understood the necessity of joining a union. But today, with the average age of a union member being mid-forties, it is evident that more needs to be done to win over youth to the cause of organised labour.

The Socialist Sunday Schools, set up as an alternative to Christian Sunday Schools in the late 1800s, attempted to attract young people to the labour movement, and even launched their own version of the Scouts called the Crusaders in 1894. The idea didn't take off. The next concerted effort came as John Hargrave left the Scouts and set up Kibbo Kift (page 14). Its denunciation of war and imperialism, promotion of outdoor living and call for world government struck a chord among socialists and trade unionists, especially in London. Many believed that Kibbo Kift could be a labour movement opposition to the imperialist Scouts of the post WWI period.

The trade unionists at the heart of this new wave were men like Joseph Reeves of the teachers' union. He and others worked closely with the Royal Arsenal Co-operative Society to form Kibbo Kift 'tribes' all over south London. These efforts came to little and could easily have become a historical footnote. However the south London 'tribes', including one fronted by Leslie Paul (page 22), left Kibbo Kift in 1924.

From 1925 the newly established Woodcraft Folk coalesced around a socialist programme that included multiple links to the trade unions, co-operatives and the Labour Party. From the beginning Woodcraft Folk supported working class struggle. In 1926, even as a tiny organisation, members attended the London demonstration supporting the General Strike.

The Seewhyer, a short-lived joint publication Co-operative Youth (CY) and Woodcraft Folk groups in Watford

Woodcraft Folk activists attend the Future That Works march, organised by the Trade Unions Congress, 20 October 2014

Over the years, Woodcraft Folk has often organised collections for strikers, but perhaps the most significant was during the miners' strike of 1984. The National Union of Miners had to take on not just the Coal Board but also Margaret Thatcher's government. With miners' families suffering real want, some Woodcraft Folk districts invited the children of miners to summer camps, in solidarity, free of charge. In 2012 Woodcraft Folk published two 'Right to Strike' guides for young members to explain what trade unions are, with suggested activities for groups.

So far the British trade union movement hasn't reciprocated in the way that, for example, Swedish unions have to their aligned youth organisation, Unga Ornar. However, there have been individual unions that have given solid support to Woodcraft Folk over the years, GMB, PCS and UNISON, for example. There are also some individual union branches that support their local Woodcraft Folk groups. While the relationship between Woodcraft Folk and unions could be stronger, both movements are, and have been since inception, united by a common cause – to create a better world for all.

More than the sum of its parts

Tracing the sometimes fraught but always strong bond between Woodcraft Folk and the wider co-operative movement

Doug Bourn
The link between Woodcraft Folk and the co-operative movement has always been more than just organisational. It has, at times, included a common vision of a just world. Leslie Paul, the co-founder of Woodcraft Folk (page 22), referred to 'working for world peace and co-operation' in his 1938 book *Republic of Children*, where he emphasised co-operation as part of a child's social and physical development. Woodcraft Folk's educational work has always exhibited strong co-operative elements, be it through camping, ceremonies or group activities.

Young Woodcraft Folk members demonstrate holding co-op placards

In the early decades of Woodcraft Folk, co-operative education was implicit. Paul would argue the best way of teaching co-operation is 'to live it'. From the 1960s onwards however, co-operation became seen as more overt. This was in part a concious response to the increasingly competitive nature of school education and the need for an alternative, but it also chimed with the emergence of an educational philosophy which emphasised child-centred learning. From the 1970s, the Woodcraft Folk constitution included developing a 'co-operative and sharing attitude to life' as a stated aim.

The most obvious example of this change of emphasis was the emergence of the new and co-operative games movement that began in North America, which had a major influence on Woodcraft Folk activities. Terry Orlick's *Co-operative Sports and Games Book*, first published in 1978, is probably the most influential example of this. Orlick argued that competition is irrational and is linked to an excessively goal orientated society. He posited that 'children nurtured on co-operation,' have a much greater chance of developing as positive and creative adults.

This more structured focus on co-operation is also reflected in a series of forward-thinking educational publications by the Woodcraft Folk in the 1980s such as *Getting On With Others*. *Let's Co-operate* also became a standard reference book for many group leaders. More recently, co-operation became the overarching theme of Woodcraft Folk's highly innovative international festival-cum-camp, CoCamp (page 184).

However, this steady growth of co-operative education has sadly not always been mirrored in the history of Woodcraft Folk's relationship with the wider co-operative movement. Although from its earliest days, Woodcraft Folk groups were supported by their local co-operative society and from 1930 by the Co-operative Union, there have been periods, most notably during and immediately after WWII, when relationships were difficult. During the war, a comparable organisation, Co-operative Youth, hoped to take over Woodcraft Folk's work. The idea was eventually rejected due to Woodcraft Folk members' fiercely independent spirit and steadfast belief in their democracy. Unfortunately the decision led to difficulties with some local co-operative societies and the Co-operative Union for a number of years.

Woodcraft Folk had the status of an auxiliary to the co-operative movement, similar to the Co-operative Women's Guild. Individual members often became active members of their local co-operative societies, joining committees and playing leading roles at a national level.

Above: A sponsored walk badge from 50th anniversary events. Top right: Gate to a village of tents at the 50th anniversary international camp held at Stanford Hall

Formal relations began to improve with the 50th anniversary international camp, which was held in 1975 at Stanford Hall, then home of the Co-operative College. For example, local co-operative societies in northern England funded the establishment of Woodcraft Folk's first regional office in Leeds in 1977. From the 1980s, the co-operative movement itself was becoming more directly involved in supporting educational programmes within schools, producing educational resource packs on co-operation for teachers. Woodcraft Folk members were involved in the drafting of these materials and the legacy of this work can be seen in the very successful co-operative schools movement.

The continued importance of co-operative learning and impact within schools is now well recognised but what has not been sufficiently well documented is the contribution Woodcraft Folk has played to this broader debate on the values of co-operative education.

Badges

The use of badges to recognise achievements in non-formal youth work is widespread beyond Woodcraft Folk. Like much scouting culture it can be traced back to the American author and naturalist Ernest Thompson Seton. Before WWI Seton created a large curriculum of 'woodcraft degrees', each with a striking abstract emblem. The requirements to obtain such a degree were challenging. 'The Camper' degree, for example, required an individual to 'light fifteen fires in succession with fifteen matches, one at least, on a wet day' and 'travel 500 miles in canoe, on foot, or in saddle, sleeping out.'

As the Scouts and Woodcraft Folk appropriated many of Seton's ideas, both established their own programme of badges. Many of the early Woodcraft Folk tests were just as rigorous as Seton's. The 1930s 'Test of the Hobo' for example required members to go on a 'seven day hike alone' and 'map all the ancient tracks and Roman roads in England.' In addition to tracking experience and skills, badges were also a way to express identity. In the 1930s members would wear a hand-made Woodcraft Folk emblem on their left breast and a bespoke badge representing their personal identity on the right breast.

As the organisation grew, individually making badges to match a centrally-set design became impractical. Woodcraft Folk began manufacturing screen printed canvas bases which members could embroider over, and later mass produced woven badges that could simply be sewn on. Over time, the designs and requirements of badges have changed significantly. As standardised testing has become ever more dominant in British schools, many Woodcraft Folk leaders have lost faith in any kind of examinations a methods of education. Whether the rigour and skillful learning the badges once offered can remain in a post-testing pedagogy is an ongoing debate in the movement.

Left column: starched screen printed bases to be embroidered over. From top to bottom:
• Self-Knowledge badge
• Social History badge
• Keen Eye badge
• Backwoodsman badge
• Long Crafter badge

Right column: mass produced fabric badges. From top to bottom:
• I Begin badge
• 1990s Ecologist badge
• 1970s Ecologist badge
• Camper badge
• Pioneer badge

A hand-made
Woodcraft Folk badge
still sewn onto the pocket
of its shirt. A yellow sun
is rising against a blue
sky which was more
common in the early
years although was
gradually replaced with
a red sun against a yellow
or orange sky. The colour
change effectively became
official following a 1946
ballot asking members
for their preference

This array of Woodcraft
Folk emblem badges
captures some of the
variations in production
and texture the symbol
has seen in its history

Brass Woodcraft Folk
single pine badge

Strong and straight like the pine

Whilst the Woodcraft Folk symbol has always been some version of two trees against a sunrise, since the early days of the organisation a metal badge showing a single pine tree has been popular. The badge is a reference to the old Elfin declaration 'I will grow strong and straight like the pine', which was discarded in the 1980s after some became worried it was not inclusive of disabled members. One of the first badges to be mass produced by Folk Supply, the single pine was originally cast in brass and hooked into the button hole of a drill shirt. Later, the badges were made with pins attached and more recently began to be produced with a silver chrome finish.

Veteran campaigner
Brian Haw, who
camped for ten years
outside the Houses of
Parliament in protest
of the invasion of Iraq,
wore Woodcraft Folk
badges, including the
single pine badge, on the
peak of his iconic hat

A Test of the Sunburnt Skin emblem drawn by the Rangers Woodcraft Folk group in their 1927 log book (page 33)

The Test of the Sunburnt Skin

Alarmingly, one of the earliest Woodcraft Folk badges, the Lone Crafter (page 139), included deliberately getting sunburnt as a required challenge. The 'Test of the Sunburnt Skin' demanded that the camper sit without a shirt for half a day to 'be sunburnt to the waist and over limbs.' Ironically the experience was intended to instil the young with knowledge of 'precautions against scorching and treatment of sunburn.' Before the link between melanoma and sunburn was fully understood it was common for exposure to the elements to be idealised in Woodcraft Folk and beyond. Readers will be relieved to learn that the Test of the Sunburnt Skin has long since been abolished from badgework.

Other tests in the Lone Crafter curriculum that revolved around self-sufficiency included keeping a four-hour vow of silence while continuing with normal camp duties and making a 10-mile solo hike while producing a map of the journey.

Painting
A depiction of a camp
by Cambridge DF
Peter Cross executed
in the style of vintage
British railway posters.
The painting was made
into a greetings postcard
for CoCamp (page 184)

A circle we'll make

As a shape and symbol, the circle holds particular significance for Woodcraft Folk. Members meet in circles, camp in circles and sing in circles. Woodcraft Folk artwork is full of refences to circles, most notably the movement's twin pine and sunrise emblem, which other than for brief periods in the 1920s and early 2000s, has consistently been circular despite many expressive iterations. In 1946, when preparing a bulk order for printed canvas versions of the emblem, the then National Council wrote to all members seeking opinions on the design. They stated that in their view that the 'symbol is enclosed in a circle – the sign of unity.'

The word 'circle' has in itself come to be synonymous with a meeting in the Woodcraft Folk lexicon. A yell of 'Circle!' when on a camp camp is a signal for all campers to gather (in a circle formation, of course) for announcements. The opening line of the most widely sung Woodcraft Folk song (page 117) runs 'Link your hands together, a circle we'll make, this bond of our friendship no power can break.'

Multiple influences have reinforced this love affair with circles. Some nomadic Native American tribes of the Great Plains arranged their tipi encampments in large circles which (via the writing of Ernest Thompson Seton) inspired many early woodcraft organisations including Woodcraft Folk's predeccesor, the Kindred of the Kibbo Kift (page 14). Also like Kibbo Kift, early Woodcraft Folk found meaning in medieval European legends. King Arthur's mythical round table, at which all knights are considered equal peers, has helped create a cultural backdrop where equality is circular. This practice was steadily reinforced by the army and the Scouts. Despite the practical uses of a circle, the Scout's pseudo-military system of ranks and strict hierarchies found physical expression in barrack-like linear camp layouts, further driving Woodcraft Folk leaders to embrace circles as an overt alternative.

Campers gather
around a fire in a circle,
the most efficient shape
for distributing heat to
everyone equally, 2012

Aerial photograph
50th anniversary
international camp,
Stamford Hall, 1975

A village circle at the
1975 international camp

Circle games take place
on Brighton beach, 1946

A large circular
camp, 1930s

Woodcraft Folk
delegation visit to
Western Sahara, 2013

Watford District form
a circle on camp, 1964

Above: Lockerbrook
activity centre in
Hope Valley,
Derbyshire.
Right: Cudham
activity centre in
Westerham, Kent

Activity centres

Dotted around the UK are Woodcraft Folk's
activity centres. From Yorkshire and the Peak
District to Kent and Suffolk these buildings
provide accommodation for groups of young
people to use as a base for adventures nearby.

Accommodation at Lockerbrook in the early years was rough. We lay on straw mattresses which we stuffed ourselves and slept on the stone slabs of the old sheep shed. We washed in the ice-cold brook down the hill – the one which gave its name to the farm. The annual camp that Basil 'Brown Eagle' Rawson ran there was different to others. His method was heuristic – we learned by doing, and we did everything: rock-climbing at Winnats Pass with real heights, bivouacking for days on the exposed peat of Kinder Scout, carrying water, food and stoves while navigating using only a compass and map.

I remember occasional scary moments when the fog descended but Rawson always knew where we were, popping up at rendezvous, or watching through his binoculars from a distant high-point. Through simple, supported endurance challenges, we learned independence and felt enabled – more equipped for life.

Martin Pover reflects on his time at Lockerbook activity centre in the 1960s as a 16 year old

Blanket toss

The time-honoured tradition of flinging someone into the air using a sudden team tug on a taut blanket is likely as old as blankets themselves. It certainly dates back to the earliest Woodcraft Folk camps and is alive and well today.

An especially impressive fling from the seventies

A child is tossed into the air from an outstretched parachute (page 98) at a training camp held at Woodcraft Folk's Park Farm activity centre in Lurgashall, September 2012

A somewhat erratic blanket toss at the 1946 internatioanl camp in Brighton (page 92)

From drill shirts to Woodies in hoodies

Expressing identity through clothing across decades of taste and technological change

Zoë Waterman

There was an urban myth circulating Woodcraft Folk districts in the eighties: A northern district was driving south down the M1 for their summer camp and a southern one heading north. They stopped at the same service station. When it was time to get back on the bus, a leader from one of the groups shouted 'Woodcraft' and rounded all the green-shirted children who replied 'Folk' onto their bus and set off down the motorway. Twenty miles down the road a small Elfin piped up, 'I don't know any of you' and the realisation of what had happened dawned – a child had inadvertently

Top: A Woody Hoody with the 'Education for Social Change' slogan. Left: A Woodcraft Folk knitted bobble hat

been scooped up by the wrong group.

While this story may be exaggerated, it tells us something about the continuing ubiquity of the green shirt in many groups in the 1980s. Cambridge member Owen Sedgwick-Jell remembers that, in his district, he was required to wear a folk shirt when travelling to camp, to aid being rounded up on train stations and in motorway service stations. They were also required wearing for council circle on camp. In the anarchistic parent-run co-operative Woodcraft Folk group I joined in the mid-eighties there were no such expectations, but if you did have a folk shirt you were only allowed to sew on three badges in the name of creating equality between those who had been members for a long time and newer additions to the group. The green drill shirt and the green T-shirt were items to be proud of, and the only Woodcraft Folk costume I came across as an Elfin. I loved my Woodcraft Folk T-shirt and wore it with pride to group nights, camps and events, but wouldn't have worn it outside a Woodcraft Folk context.

In the late eighties, changes in technology meant that it became cost-effective to do short print runs of different clothing designs. This, along with hand printed and drawn designs from specific groups, led to an explosion of different Woodcraft Folk clothing. T-shirts from camps became a badge of honour; like a fading gig T-shirt of your favourite band, they joined other colourful designs for anniversaries and events that people would wear as a fashion item, outside Woodcraft Folk sessions, in the wider world. The District Fellows (page 188) often led the way with these new designs – bringing the expertise of young artists, theatre designers, architects, tailors and other budding creative professionals to bear on the development of Woodcraft Folk costume culture.

In the late 1990s DFs created what was to herald a major shift in Woodcraft Folk wear, which tuned in with the youth fashion of the time. At a DF Committee meeting in a house in Bath, the 'Woody Hoody' was born. Plates of different sizes were taped onto someone's back to establish the optimum size for the emblem which was this was then drawn up by Sheffield DF, Alex Wilde. Meanwhile Hornsey member, Bronia Housman designed an arrangement of the motto 'Education for Social Change' for the front of the hoody. Initially the hoodies were printed in small runs, marketed through the internal publication *DF News*, and sold out of a Cambridge DF's house. Soon sheer number being ordered, from all parts of the organisation became unmanageable as boxes of hoodies stacked up. Woodcraft Folk's long-standing central kit producer, Folk Supply, stepped in to take on their production and sale.

Continued on page 169

1920s
Hand-made long
sleeved felt jerkin with
rectangular leather
Woodcraft Folk badge
and leather fringing

1930s
Short sleeved folk jerkin with leather trim and embroidered sleeves and collar. Note the handmade Woodcraft Folk badge and blackletter font shoulder tabs

1960s
Long sleeved drill
shirt typical of
postwar Woodcraft
Folk costume, highly
customised with
multiple badges

1980s
Woodcraft Folk leader
Tracy 'Crazy Horse'
Cleveland's drill shirt

1990s
Jonny Helm's Pioneer
sweatshirt featuring
the camp badge from
Sust'n'Able (page 174)

2000s
Zip-up fleeces
became popular after the
millennium and are still
sold by Folk Supply

2010s
Isabel 'Apple Belle'
Cleveland's Elfin t-shirt

2010s
Woody Hoody
featuring Bronia
Housman's
arrangement of the '
Education for Social
Change' motto

Whether wearing a classic drill shirt, green sweater, Woody Hoody, one of myriad T-shirts or their own clothes, the costume of Woodcraft Folk members has come to be as diverse and inclusive as the movement itself

As hoodies were pretty omnipresent in the early 2000s, they soon took over from the drill shirt as the most widely worn piece of Woodcraft Folk costume and marked its final move from something only worn at Woodcraft Folk events to something that was worn all over the place. In the 2003 feature documentary *Jeremy Hardy vs. the Israeli Army*, following the International Solidarity Movement and their activities in Palestine, Emma Bleach, then a DF, is seen wearing her Woody Hoody whilst acting as a human shield in Palestine.

Most Woodcraft Folk groups now would be unrecognisable to the Elfin in the green drill shirt on the wrong bus travelling to another group's camp. There is no longer an expectation that members will wear costume, and if they do there is a wide range in a rainbow of colours available. The drill shirt still exists – I wear mine to group night every week and our Elfins and Pioneers treasure the few child-sized ones that are handed down – but now there's a wide range of merchandise, it is less of a uniform and more of an affirmative choice. It is a badge of belonging, a visual confirmation of the values and a celebration of the organisation as a whole.

Venturer Camp T-shirt
by Phineas Harper, 2013

T-shirts

The humble T-shirt has transformed fashion across the world. Originating as functional military underwear, they didn't become widely popular until after WWII when United States veterans would wear them combined with civilian clothes. Lightweight, cheap and simple enough to print onto easily, T-shirts have changed the nature of Woodcraft Folk's approach to clothing.

Instead of personalising individual garments, T-shirts allowed expressive designs to be produced in small quantities to mark certain camps or events. The advent of portable screen printers meant custom T-shirts could even be produced by hand at the camp itself. As a result, the expression of identity through Woodcraft Folk clothing has partially shifted from customising a base uniform to collecting, designing and cherishing a number of unique items which resonate with cherished memories.

T-shirt by Bronwen
Thomas, 1988

London Camp T-shirt
screen printed by hand
at the camp, 1998

Top left: DF Camp
T-shirt by Aidan
Farrow, 2004

Top right: T-shirt by
Martha Radice, 1990

Bottom: T-shirt by
Phineas Harper, 2012

Sust 'n' Able 2001

Never afraid of a bad pun, in 2001 Woodcraft Folk launched Sust 'n' Able, an educational programme culminating in an international camp of 4,000 people held in Sherwood Forest, Nottingham. The camp was themed around sustainability and included a week-long, camp-wide project drafting a declaration targeted at world leaders meeting at the United Nations World Summit on Sustainable Development the following year. The final declaration was presented to the UN by a delegation of eleven young people from Woodcraft Folk and IFM-SEI (page 70) who travelled to Johannesburg for the summit.

Two-tone ska reggae band Ska Wars play the main stage

Above: A group tour the Sherwood Forest site by pedal taxi
Left: Stanwell leader Trevor Baker walks across the site with his guide dog

Sust and Able, the mascots of the 2001 international camp

Cartoon
The Guardian's political catoonist Steve Bell has been a Woodcraft Folk supporter for many years. His cartoons generally lampoon British politicians but from time to time he has made drawings which celebrate Woodcraft Folk's work such as this one from January 1990

When we were little all the normal kids went to Scouts or Brownies.
We went to Woodcraft

Where we learnt how to build homeless shelters,

Don't forget to use the bin bag to waterproof it!

And what it might feel like to be blind.

But all I wanted was to wear a uniform in a single-sex club and to pledge my allegiance to God and the Queen.

There is no way I'm sending you to Brownies to wear a uniform in a single-sex club and to pledge your allegiance to God and the Queen!

© Karrie Fransman 2008

Cartoon
By Karrie Fransman.
First published in *The Guardian*, 15 July 2008

Top: Three campers
set up a stall for an
international fete
held at the festival

Bottom: A mug
from Tillyards Coffee,
a satirical coffee chain
which ran at the camp

Global Village 2006

Writing for *The Guardian* in August 2006,
journalist John Vidal described an event 'mixing
the spirit of Glastonbury, the concerns of the
UN and the passion of the playground'. He
was referring to Global Village, a 5000-strong
international camp hosted by Woodcraft Folk
in Kent. The festival was themed around the
Millennium Development Goals with an expansive
programme of diverse activities from a solar
cinema, to wood-fired sauna to a satirical coffee
house chain run as a members' co-operative.
More than 50 countries sent delegations
to Global Village making it one of the most
international events Woodcraft Folk has hosted.

Top: Three Sri Lankan
boys in a Vango tent.
They camped with
Wimbledon district

Bottom: Issa Lo from
a Senegalese delegation
teaches drums to Fred
Harper from Wales

Vennies

The first large Woodcraft Folk camp after the 2008 financial crash was Venturer Camp 2010, conceived as an independent state, 'Vtopia'. To explore the global economic chaos, the camp used Vennies, an alternative currency which could be exchanged for food, drink and physical goods at on-camp cafes. Throughout the week the supply of Vennies was artificially distorted with crashes, hyper inflation and quantitative easing staged by the organisers to teach attendees about real world economic events and satirise neoliberal financial markets.

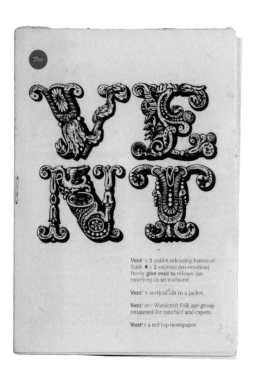

The Vent

Mini newspaper of Venturer Camp 2013, *The Vent*, was produced at The Underground Printing Press, an on-camp print workshop before being cut, folded, stapled and distributed by hand using the camp postal service

Poster

Poster designed using wood block lettering by Jonny Helm. Printed at The Underground Printing Press at Venturer Camp 2013

Below: Young member speaking at a rainbow pride procession

Right: Woven CoCamp wristband for security

CoCamp 2011

In the run-up to the UN International Year of Co-operatives, Woodcraft Folk hosted one of their most ambitious large camps to date, CoCamp. The whole event was organised as a giant co-operative in which attendees were able to shape and participate in a decentralised festival organised into four towns complete with libraries, town halls, grocers and local democracy, all under canvas. The festival brought together young people from all over the world, and featured a radio station, TV channel and its own newspaper.

A CoCamp delegate
from Palestine joins
a discussion about the
Israeli occupation

The Courier, CoCamp's
newspaper was written,
printed and distributed
to campers daily

The *Courier* newspaper.
The issue on top
is issue five, published
in Autumn 2013

The Courier

The first full-colour Woodcraft Folk newspaper
was inspired by a daily newspaper of the same
name which had opened at Woodcraft Folk's
2011 international festival of co-operation,
CoCamp (page 184). It was produced by the same
team of young members with a strong graphic
and editorial resemblance between the two
publications. The paper included a mix of internal
and external stories with news, opinions pieces,
group activities, reports from overseas volunteers,
thematic features and occasional high-profile
guest columnists including Labour and Green
Party MPS. *The Courier* sought contributions from
across the organisation, giving space to young
children and experienced older adult leaders.

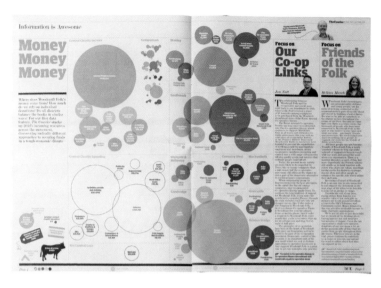

Spreads from issues five
(top) and six (bottom)
of *The Courier*, 2013

Where youth and adulthood collide

A movement in a movement, the rise of DFs, Woodcraft Folk's eldest young people

Joel White
At the time of publication District Fellows (DFs), the 16-20 age group of Woodcraft Folk, is 39 years old yet as youthful as ever running groups for younger children and playing a national role self-organising events, projects and activities. Mooted in a 1977 letter to Woodcraft Folk National Council by Education Committee member Jess Cawley, 'District Fellowships' were officially inaugurated at the Annual Delegates Conference of April that year, the same month that The Clash released their eponymous debut album. Records of DF affairs in those days of punk and a dying post-war consensus are hard to come by, but things start surfacing again in the 1980s as members begin to construct the organisation on more autonomous grounds, helped on many

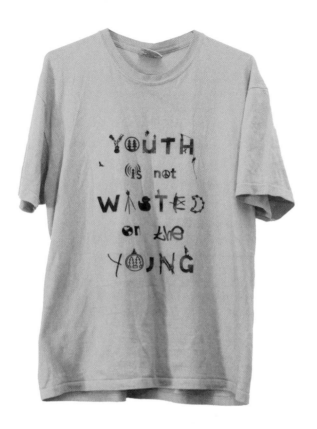

DF T-shirt designed
by Phineas Harper
and Joel White, 2011

accounts by the support of part-time Woodcraft
Folk employee Michael Bond. The first iterations
of what were to become enduring DF events
happen around this time; Winter Wonderland, DF
Conference (later renamed Althing) and DF Camp.

The 1995 international camp provided a
catalyst for a national DF conscience, prefiguring
various movement-wide initiatives that continue
to this day. 'Gay Day', for example, sowed the
seeds for the 'Rainbow Network' peer education
project. By 1998 DFs were running Summer
Madness, an annual music festival which Amy
Winehouse, among many others, performed at
in 2001. The spirit of organising ambitious gigs
continued with 'Span The World With Music', a
string of pop-up mini festivals founded in 2009.
The post-millennial DFs of my own era saw a

focus on collective identity, expressive branding, consensus-building and campaigns against nuclear weapons and climate change, alongside huge efforts of organisation towards camps for peers and younger Woodcraft Folk members alike. DFs has always been a platform for the contestation of political issues as they pique in public discourse, often exposing wider Woodcraft Folk to new arguments within liberation struggles.

The story of DFs exposes us to the contingent quality of youth itself, which in our era of precarious work, housing crises, education privatisation, and political anxiety, seems to be under threat as a space for creativity, expression and collective knowledge. In a smaller but just as profound way, DF experience is made up of the thousands of personal moments of care, camping, hilarity, discussion and abandon that can't be captured in a traditional summary. The muddy night-long jungle raves, the wild wide games, the long meetings, the costumes, the thousands of interpersonal sparks and friendships. Whether we freeze these moments, or let them drift in a happy haze, DFs has been a formative threshold for generations of Woodcraft Folk – a bubbling island of collectivity, situated at the moment when youth and adulthood collide.

Natalie Bennett, leader of the Green Party in England and Wales speaks on a panel of politicians in a debate at DF Camp 2013, chaired by London DF, Jess Poyner

Above: One of many
DF Camp night-long
raves: costumes, face
paint, glitter and shape-
throwing aplenty, 2013.
Right: The DF emblem
is a basic, two trees in
a circle, shape which
any member can adapt,
and rework. This badge
version was embroidered
by Kezia Harper in 2008

Ninety years young

The 90th anniversary heritage project

Nicola Samson

In 1935, Woodcraft Folk's 10th souvenir edition of *The Pioneer* (page 76), marked the organisation's 10th anniverary. The 25th was commemorated in *The Helper* (page 78); the 40th brought an anniversary dinner, and the 50th an international camp of thousands. Founding Woodcraft Folk member Leslie Paul (page 22) spoke at a 60th anniversary conference. Badges, books, banners, songs, films, floral displays and not least T-shirts (page 170) have marked many an anniversary, and the early years of the 21st century produced Woodcraft Folk's first heritage website. At each milestone, not least the 90th anniversary heritage project, of which this book is part, a core intention was to bring its past

Hand in hand, together in friendship, through the decades towards a new and peaceful world into the present; to stimulate and record memories, and inspire members to explore Woodcraft Folk's rich history and its relationship to the organisation's future. The project included recording oral history interviews with adult members which have been added to the British Library Sound Archive, young children creating history scrapbooks, the introduction of a new heritage badge, the production of a documentary film, a touring exhibition which opened at London's City Hall and a vast process of cataloguing and archiving historical artefacts, without which these pages would not have been possible. Building on the extraordinary range of projects marking the first 90 years of Woodcraft Folk, the movement looks forward to 100.

Painting
By Watford member,
Eric Beal, 1949

The 200 pages you hold in your hand are the product of a
vast process of rummaging through cardboard boxes, hunting
in attics, researching, cataloguing, photographing, designing and
story-telling all carried out in an ambitiously tight time-frame.
We couldn't have done it without some very special individuals.
The editorial board and I would like to say a massive thank you
to the host of people who have helped in small and colossal
ways to make this publication possible. In particular I want
to thank the awesome Jonny Helm whose credit as our
photographer does little to capture the enthusiastic, gracious,
diplomatic and organisational tour de force he has been.
Also Annebella Pollen and Martin Pover, two crucial volunteers
who gave up weekends, evenings and brain-space to write,
tweak and advise throughout the journey. Thank you – this
project wouldn't have half the subtlety, humour and richness
without your generous, tireless input.

Thank you to all of those named on the masthead (page 2),
the proof readers, researchers, graphic designer and printers.
Special thanks to Deborah McCahon, Sarah McDonell, Jon Nott,
Nicola Samson and the wider Woodcraft Folk staff team who
solved many problems behind the scenes. More thank yous to
Amica Dall, Jane Hall and Anthony Engi Meacock of architecture
practice Assemble for their advice, insight and on more than
one occasion providing a base for me to work from. Likewise
to Luke Freedman whose wisdom helped shape the editorial
direction early on. To Anna Towlson from the London School
of Economics library and her team who store and protect
many of the artifacts shown in these pages and who were
exceptionally helpful arranging visits to the LSE reading room
and Tim Turner, a collector of Kibbo Kift artefacts.

Thank you to my mother, Meg for arranging for the set of
carved staffs on page 55 to make their way to London for
photographing. Thanks also to my father, Alan who, like an
over-equipped wizard, couriered the staffs to London by train
on the eve of his own mother's birthday. From the Architecture
Foundation, I am grateful to Ellis Woodman for accommodating

my (many) requests for leave to work on the book and to curator Matthew Bovingdon-Downe who patiently rescheduled numerous meetings in the run-up to publication.

Thank you to Tracy, Ian, Isabelle and Scott Cleveland who donated a host of contemporary artifacts. To Joan Pover who dug out her amazing scale model tent (page 108) and was a constant source of memories. To Nick Parsons and Ralph Blackbourn who threw together make-shift studios with impressive speed when we urgently needed a hoody shot. I would also like to specifically thank a number of Woodcraft Folk members: Andrew Bibby, Monica Eady, Andrew Flinn, Veronica Hammerstone, Richard Kirkwood, Lloyd Russell-Moyle, Gill Norris, Rich Palser, Tamsin Pearce, Chris Pyke, Julie Thorpe all of whom helped tie down facts and stories.

We're grateful to the Heritage Lottery Fund for helping fund this project and to the Arts and Humanities Research Council for funding the reproduction of several key photographs and Annebella Pollen's research time.

I'd like to say a personal thank you to my partner Saskia Neibig for supporting and advising me through many long nights of editing and to my former colleagues from *The Architectural Review*, Julia Dawson, Alex Ecob, Will Hunter, Cath Slessor and Tom Wilkinson, whose many graphic and grammatical lessons run throughout these pages. I also want to thank Veronica Jones, Kit Jones and Tom Dunhill whose friendship and leadership have guided and inspired me during my time in Woodcraft Folk.

Many thanks to Jeremy Corbyn for generously contributing the foreword (page 6) and to Nadine Spencer and Jack Bond who helped make that possible.

Finally, a massive shout-out to the 424 members of the People's History of Woodcraft Folk Facebook group who crowd-sourced memories, facts, pictures, stories and nuggets of history at every stage of the journey.

Artefacts

All artefacts included in this book were photographed by Jonny Helm and were supplied courtesy of Woodcraft Folk except where listed otherwise below

Doves is a font revived by Robert Green based on Punchcutter, Edward Prince's 1899 typeface for Doves Press of London. Punchcutter was almost lost forever after Doves Press co-founder, Thomas James Cobden-Sanderson dumped the entire lead type set into the River Thames from Hammersmith Bridge in a dispute. In 2014 Green led a diving expedition to recover pieces of the lost font and has since produced a digital version from studying the lead originals. Published by Typespec.

Gill Sans was created by the sculptor, print maker and socialist Eric Gill. It takes inspiration from calligrapher Edward Johnston's 1916 'Underground Alphabet', the font which is used throughout the London Underground network. Published by Monotype.

'It is not enough to do as we do because we did. We must know what we do and why we do it.'

Leslie Paul, 1928

Speed the adventure...